CREATOR

SUSTAINER

PROTECTOR

الله
GOD

Sheikh and Disciple

Sheikh
and
Disciple

by

His Holiness
M. R. Bawa Muhaiyaddeen

THE FELLOWSHIP PRESS
Philadelphia, PA

Library of Congress Cataloging in Publication Data

Muhaiyaddeen, M. R. Bawa.
    The sheikh and disciple.

    1. Sufism--Addresses, essays, lectures. I. Title.
BP189.62.M627 1983   297'.4   83-1565
ISBN 0-914390-26-0

Printed in the United States of America
First Printing 1983
Second Printing 1992

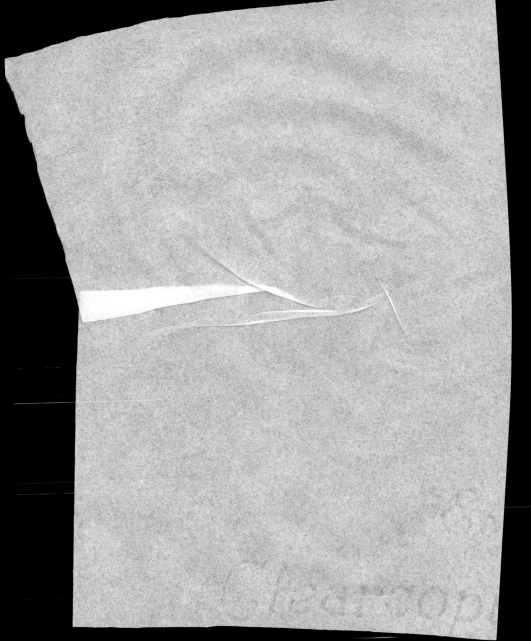

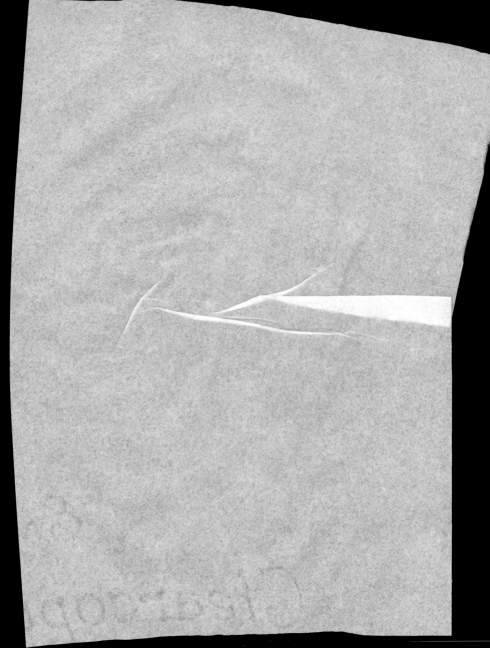

About the Author

M. R. Bawa Muhaiyaddeen is a revered sage and holy man who emerged from the jungles of Sri Lanka in 1914. Little is known of his history prior to this time, except that he traveled extensively throughout the Middle East and India. He has spent his entire life as a student of the world's religions and an observer of the subtle secrets of God's creation.

For the past fifty years, His Holiness has been sharing these experiences with thousands of people from all over the world. Though he teaches within the framework of Islamic Sufism, people from the Christian, Judaic, and Hindu faiths also come to him in their search for wisdom. Respected by scholars and leaders of various philosophies and spiritual traditions, His Holiness has the unique ability to distill the essential truth from all religions and to renew faith within the hearts of men.

Responding to the invitation of several individuals, His Holiness first came to the United States in 1971. During His subsequent visits to this country he has

peared on many television and radio programs and
as spoken on university campuses throughout the
United States and Canada. The author of over twenty
books, His Holiness has also been the subject of num-
erous newspaper and magazine articles including
Time, *Psychology Today*, and *The Harvard Divinity
Bulletin*.

Acknowledgments

The Sheikh and Disciple is a special collection of discourses spoken by His Holiness M. R. Bawa Muhaiyaddeen in Colombo, Sri Lanka. These talks were originally given to a small group of individuals who had gathered from all corners of the globe, from the United States, Canada, Mexico, South Africa, England, Germany, Australia, and India. They came to gain a greater understanding of the connection between man and God, through the example and tutelage of a realized teacher. This book describes the role and duty of such a teacher and serves as a gauge by which the disciple can measure his focus and progress on the path.

Originally spoken in Tamil, an ancient Dravidian language found in Southern India and Sri Lanka, these talks were spontaneously translated into English by Dr. and Mrs. K. Ganesan. They were then transcribed and edited into book form. All those who worked on this project humbly ask forgiveness for any loss of clarity or vitality in this transition from spoken to written word.

May God bless this venture and all those who read this book. *Āmīn.*

Contents

Introduction

My love you, my grandchildren, my daughters and sons, brothers and sisters. May Allah, to whom all praise and praising belong, show us the way to a life of purity. May He prove to us the wealth of truth in our lives. May He show us proof of our connection with Him and of the unity between us, and may He help us to attain that state in our lifetime. *Amīn.*

My children, for what reason have we gathered here together? One reason is love. Another is to discover a way to find peace for our hearts and, in the time between our birth and our death, to discover the connection between God and man so that we can end the suffering in this life. These are the reasons we are here now.

We have gathered here because we have been searching for a man of wisdom for many long days, months, and years, hoping that if we found such a good and wise man we could then understand our connection with God. Some will love this man of wisdom as a father. Some will love him as a grand-

1

father. For some, the relationship to him will be that of a brother, sister, child, or grandchild. Some children may call him a sheikh, others may call him a guru. They may address him in many ways. But no matter what they call him, they will have all gathered in love and unity.

For a father, there is only one point—whether the children are young or old, they are all his children. He addresses them all as "my children." Where do these words come from? They come from his heart. He gave birth to these children from his heart. They are never separate from him; they are always a part of his love, a part of his qualities, and a part of his compassion. There is no separation between the father and the children. He shows no differences toward any of them. He teaches them wisdom according to their qualities, conduct, actions, and maturity. The father gives his children the food and protection they need.

Children, you should never think you are being treated differently from the others. Do not make your different needs into differences among yourselves. Only a man of wisdom can know how to judge the needs of each child. Since you do not have that ability, you cannot fathom how much is needed. Think about this. You must not harbor doubts, thinking the father is giving more food to one child or more wisdom to another. Never judge like that.

Do not keep such doubt within you. Doubt kills wisdom, love, faith, compassion, and unity. Ignorance can be dispelled by wisdom, but doubt is very difficult to drive away. It is easy for moonlight to dispel the darkness, but when the moon is covered by clouds it is difficult for its light to penetrate. Even sunlight finds it difficult to penetrate. Doubts are like those clouds; it is difficult for wisdom to break through them. But when there are no clouds, the light can shine directly.

If one has the qualities of doubt, suspicion, or jealousy, it is difficult for wisdom, love, and faith to dispel them from the heart. Ignorance can easily be dispelled, but it is very difficult to break through these other qualities. If you want to go on this path, you should not have such thoughts. A man of wisdom will know what you need. He will watch as you progress step by step and will give to you according to your level of maturity. A wise father will know. Every child should think about this.

My love you, my grandchildren, my brothers and sisters. There are many different kinds of learning on this path. Some learning has to be done on the earth, some in the sea, some in the air, some in the sky. Other learning must be done within the body of man. I too had to learn all this myself. I will tell you of certain experiences in my life.

First I had to learn about the ether, the sky, the section above the head. Ether can conceal the self. There are many clouds, many colors, many hues, many suns, moons, stars, thunder and lightning, rain, gales, and storms overhead. All that is above the mind is like ether. So much exists beyond the mind; there are four hundred trillion, ten thousand different sections. Energies, cells, viruses, spirits, *saktis,* illusion, darkness, torpor—whatever is beyond the control of the mind is like the ether or sky. But once you control these energies with wisdom, they become like the earth. Once you can control the thoughts of the mind, you are treading on earth. If we can control what is above us and bring it under our feet, then we can learn.

Next I went to the jungle. Some people go to live in caves, some go to the Himalaya mountains or to other isolated places. I was told that if I went to such a place I could meditate in peace. "Is that so?" I said. "I must go and see." And so I went to the jungle. There I found snakes, insects, flowers, jungle fowl, and all sorts of animals. I discovered that all the sections in the world are even more prevalent in the jungle. All around me there were lions, tigers, wild horses, pigs, foxes, and dogs. They ran about, hunted for food, and slept. Some animals came out in the night, some in the daytime. Some animals caught and ate each other. Some ran in fear of the others. This is what I saw in the jungle.

I lived there among the animals. I lived in the caves where they lived. I roamed the way they roamed, and I climbed the trees they climbed. Without any separation I drank beside them from the ponds. I mingled with them and studied their qualities, actions, feelings, intellect, and awareness. I learned from each creation. I found that the jungle is not a place of peace in which to meditate; it belongs to the animals. I learned that the animals behave in the jungle just like people behave in the world. Animals live in caves; man sits in caves. Animals go out in search of food; man goes out and takes whatever he sees. Animals have not discovered anything about man, nor has man discovered anything about himself. How can one who has not discovered what is within man meditate? In this way I studied the beings in the jungle, and then I left.

Next I studied the creatures of the ocean. They too were behaving in the same way. I finished that lesson and began to study birds. They were also the same. Some ate fruit, some ate worms, some ate insects, some killed one another. One variety ate dead animals, another ate live ones. They built nests, laid eggs, and hatched them. I watched and studied all their qualities and actions.

Then I came to the city and studied the animals there. I discovered that human animals were behaving just like other creatures. Whatever qualities these other beings had, man also had. What the monkey had, man had. What the venomous snake had, man had. The human animal was not a wonder. He did not have anything different from the animals.

At this point I realized that the most difficult task in life is to find a true man among the created beings. To find a true human being and to understand him is very difficult indeed. Only after realizing the true man and God within myself could I perform true meditation. I had to understand the cage of this body. Outer acts are not real. I had to find the place within to perform true meditation.

At this point I was told, "There is a house that was built and given to you. That house is your body."

"But this body is only eight spans," I said. "How can I live here?"

5

Then He told me, "Even an ant's body is eight spans of its own hand. The body is a school. It is your house, your heaven, your hell, and My kingdom. Your freedom is there, yet your slavery is also there. Both your joys and your sorrows are there. Man-animal and Man-God are both there. All this learning is within the eight-span house of your body. If you become an *insān,* a true man, you will understand this. You are a secret. I am a Mystery."

According to His words, I started to learn about the cage of my body. Within this eight-span body, I set out to discover what should be discarded and what should be taken in. I was told, "Within this eight-span house, half a span is your sorrow, half a span is your torpor, and one span is the fire of hell. If you can understand and discard these two spans, then you are left with six. Once you have understood all that is within the remaining six spans of your body, you can become a man with six levels of wisdom, capable of analyzing and discovering the secrets of the eighteen thousand universes. Then you will understand that one handful of earth which is your heart.

"If you do not reach this understanding, you could become a worm in hell with only one level of wisdom. Or you could become a jinn, a fairy, a ghost, or a demon. You will become a *rūhani,* an elemental spirit. However, if you understand yourself, then you can become a true human being. You can become My messenger, you can become My light, you can merge with Me and we can live together." These were His words.

We have to discover what is hidden within this body. This is what we must learn from a wise man of purity. We must learn this from a pure father who has a pure heart. To do this, your unity and faith must be strong. Children, you must have purity of heart to learn from the purity of the father. The secret of God, our Father who is purity, must be learned with pure love, pure faith, pure compassion, pure unity, and a pure life. This is the only way we can learn and understand that purity, that meditation, that prayer, and that learning.

If each one of you establishes and understands this state within, then the connection between you and your Father can easily be established. You can conduct your lives with ease and understand all you need to know. You can understand the life in which wisdom, good deeds, our Father, and the children live together. When love, wisdom, and unity are all together, that is the heaven of *gnānam.* The children of the pure Father will live in the paradise of *gnānam.* That is *firdaus,* our Father's pure kingdom. We will be given the radiant kingdom of our Father as our prize.

You must understand this pure place. When you can establish this within yourself and demonstrate proof of its existence, then your Father's kingdom of wisdom, love, compassion, peace, and *īmān* becomes yours.

These are some of the things I have learned through experience. My love you. Think about this. May Allah help you. *Āmīn.*

The Value of the True Sheikh

My children, my daughters and my sons, you are now traveling on the journey of your life, from the east to the west. You are traveling across a huge ocean of illusion, through jungles, deserts, and forests. This is the journey of life on which you will experience many difficulties, joys, sorrows, losses, heaven, and hell. My children, there is a reason for undertaking this journey. You are in search of something.

On the path to God, there is only one point in life, there is only one thing to search for—wisdom. You must proceed on this journey searching for wisdom, and you must attain the liberation of your soul. You must cross over the sea of illusion, the sea of desire, the arid desert where nothing grows, the mind and dreams which are barren, and the jungle filled with animals. There is nothing to be seen in all this. These places only exist in the mind, and you must go beyond them all. To do this, you need a *gnāna* sheikh. Only a sheikh can point the way to God through the use of a special map.

As you proceed on this journey, you will encounter many difficulties and sorrows. There will be blood-ties and differences of race and religion. However, when faced with these difficulties, those who are immersed within the sea of illusion will not realize that anything is wrong; instead, they will perceive it as comfort. The insects, worms, and viruses that live in the desert are comfortable because they are accustomed to that environment. Similarly, the monkey mind does not recognize the difficulties of the jungle; it has always lived there and knows nothing else. Human animals also know nothing other than this jungle. But a true man should understand these things.

If man wants to find the joy of the liberated soul of life, then he must proceed on this journey. Along the way he will encounter a desert, barren, without grass or weeds. The heat of the sun will be scorching, but in the midst of this barren wilderness there will be a tree. As soon as he sees that tree the traveler will run beneath it. Immediately he will realize the comfort and peace which the shade provides, and his fatigue will be relieved. Once he experiences the peace and comfort of the shade, he will never leave the tree to return to the hot sun.

Many forms of life can be found both on and beneath that tree. There are insects, germs, and viruses that live on the leaves, branches, and bark. Do they realize the comfort which the tree provides? No, they do not. Life is always the same for them. They do not know the difference between joy and sorrow. Only someone who has undergone this journey and has known the dangers of being exposed to the hot sun will realize the comfort of the shade. Only he will know the true value of that tree.

The search for a sheikh, for God, and for truth is also like this. On the journey of your life, as soon as you find this shade, your sadness, sorrows, and difficulties will immediately leave. You will experience peace, tranquillity, and serenity. If you find such a place, you will find peace. But that search and determination must be there.

If you make the effort, you will find comfort and peace from the shade. Later, relieved of your fatigue, you can once again continue on your journey. When the heat lessens and the sun goes down, the sheikh will say, "Now you can proceed. Your journey will be much easier now. Come, let us go. Now that it is cool, we can cross this desert. We must go beyond this mirage to the other side." The sheikh will then take you across the desert to a cool place.

It is necessary that we experience certain hardships on this journey. Those who have not suffered and undergone these difficulties and who simply find themselves in the comfort of the shade, like those who are always with the sheikh, will not recognize the benefits. They are like the leaves, beetles, and insects who are living on the tree without realizing its value. They need to be aware of the heaviness and weariness of life. Then, with wisdom and determination, they must make the effort to purify their souls. They must truly know that they need God, and knowing this, they must make the effort to end their sorrows.

If people can understand both the troubles they experienced earlier in their lives and the comfort and joy experienced later after meeting the sheikh, then they will realize the true value of the sheikh. Without this awareness, they will never understand the joys and sorrows of this journey. Although they are with the sheikh, they are like the beetle that does not know the preciousness of the shade. They do not know that on this journey there is great value to be found—shade is given, fatigue is relieved, and great benefits are obtained.

Even though many children have been with the *gnāna* sheikh for a long time, if they do not have the correct focus, if they do not experience the joys and sorrows, and if they do not have certitude and determination, there is absolutely no use in their being with such a teacher. Like beetles, these children just fly in circles and return to rest on the same branch; they do not progress on their journey. They are like insects feeding upon the world. But when the true traveler sits in the shade of the sheikh after his long journey, he is comforted. He receives rest and peace and then proceeds on this journey.

A true sheikh is one who shades and comforts the travelers crossing the desert of this world. In this barren desert of illusion all that exists is a mirage. You see this mirage and run toward it searching for water, but it is just a dream. However, at that very moment when you are confused and entranced by this mirage, you will find a tree nearby which can provide shade. That tree is the sheikh.

Life is a desert. People are suffering and the

13

sheikh is there to soothe them and lend a helping hand. If you have the longing and determination to go on this journey, if you are in the proper state and know what you are searching for, then no matter how hard it may become, the sheikh can help ease the difficulties, the sorrows, and the fatigue you experience.

You must recognize the value of the sheikh and the work which he has come to do. Once you realize this, you can be comforted by him and continue on your journey. If you do not realize this, you will be like the insects on that tree who do not know the value of shade and have no purpose in life. Such people do not know what the sheikh's work is or the peace he can give. Please think about this.

You must realize: ''The sheikh has helped me to dispel so much suffering and sadness. So many problems have been cleared because of his help. How much peace I have gained on this journey of my life, and how much more he will help me to proceed even further.'' If you have the determination to search for God, then you will understand the value of this shade in the midst of the desert.

Consider another point. When you come to a sheikh, how must you behave? Depending on your behavior, the sheikh will use one of two terms to describe you—a clever child or a fool. Let me explain. This world is like a huge bale of cotton. It is very bulky but almost weightless. You can tie up bags and bags of cotton and fill huge shiploads, but it has little value. Even though it occupies so much space, it takes just one tiny spark of fire to destroy it all. In comparison, a gem is very small. It does not occupy much space yet it has great value.

Like this, no matter how many things you gather during your lifetime, they are all dreams which can be destroyed as easily as cotton wool. This dream world consists of all that you collect in your life. But when you take a good look, it is only cotton wool. One small spark of fire will destroy it all.

A sheikh has the fire of wisdom, and with that he can burn everything you bring with you. You must be careful about bringing him things that can be consumed by this fire. All the bundles you have collected in your life, all the thoughts of races, religion, and bloodties, and all your attachments can be burned by this fire of wisdom.

You carry all these bundles which are suitable only for the garbage truck. They can be destroyed with one spark of the fire of wisdom. You have four hundred trillion, ten thousand different kinds of cotton which you bring here in shiploads. Your work is to load and unload and carry all these bundles. You waste all your time doing this. You tie them in bundles and load them on the ship. Then you unload the ship, and later load it again! But the sheikh does not load and unload these things. He can destroy them all very easily with one spark of that fire.

The whole world, this body, and this life are burdens. You see this world as something huge, but it is only a dream. You are taken in by all the dreams you see, but they are only mirages. The world is a desert of illusion, yet you try to grab everything you see. You think this will quench your thirst, but you

15

will never be able to drink from this mirage. You will never find relief there. Your body is small; in comparison, the world is much bigger. But your mind is even bigger than the world, your desire is even bigger than your mind, and all your karma is still greater than that. This is the sum total of your dreams. These things are useless to you. When you go to a sheikh all these have to be burned away.

There is something very small within you. Truth is very, very small, but like the gem, it is very heavy and very valuable. Unlike the cotton wool, that truth has great weight. The wisdom of the sheikh is like that truth, very tiny and very heavy. When the sheikh gives you this, you must receive it very carefully and delicately. You must realize the immense value of what he gives and have the strength to bear its great weight. The strength of faith, determination, and certitude must develop within. You must stretch out your hand with that strength of certitude and accept what the sheikh gives. You must realize that it will be heavy, and you must have the strength to bear that weight. If you do not, you will be unable to carry it. If you are already carrying one burden and try to take on yet another burden, you are likely to drop them both. Or if you are daydreaming while reaching for this gift, it may fall and you may fall too.

So, how should you receive this gift? You should gather all your strength and reach out your hand. You must be strong enough. You must fully understand the profound weight of what the sheikh is giving. If you receive it in this way, you will be able to hold onto it when it is placed in your hands. Then, when you place it in your *qalb,* it will have great value.

You must receive this treasure with a sharp focus, knowing its full weight and true value. You must keep it safely in the proper place. If you receive this gift and put it away carefully, the sheikh will say you are a clever child and that you are wise for treating it correctly. But if you are careless and receive it playfully, you will fall down and the gift will break. Then he will say you are a fool. The sheikh will use either of these two terms. If you realize the value of this treasure and receive it in a proper way, he will call you a wise person, a good child; but if you drop it without realizing its value, he will say you are a fool, that you have missed the point and have not understood its value. He will use either of these two terms depending upon your actions. You must understand this.

Whatever the sheikh gives you is very heavy. With faith, certitude, and determination, muster the strength to receive this weight and keep it carefully within you. You must take what he gives, guard it, and preserve it. You have to think about this.

You are with the sheikh now. You came here in search of something, and you must take what you came for. Every word the sheikh utters is of some value to you. Every point he makes is valuable; within his every act, his every look, there is something valuable. Every time he takes someone's hand, there is something of value in that. Every time he puts his hand on someone's head, there is some value in it. Whatever way he looks at you or touches you, there is something to it; there is a definite reason for his doing so. Something may be wrong with your blood, your nerves, or your bones. He does not touch anyone without a reason. You must think, "There is something to this." Maybe there is something wrong with your mind. There may be some lust, anger, miserliness, sexual desire, or sexual arts. He will place his hand on you to make this leave.

In whatever the sheikh does there is always some value, a deeper meaning than meets the eye. He may be cutting away a certain tendency or action, or perhaps a thought. Only the sheikh knows why he is doing this. There is always a reason. It is a secret. You must recognize its value; only then will you understand the point of what he does. Because his words and actions have such profound meaning, you must always submit to him and be vigilant to receive whatever he gives.

Yet, my children, even though you are sitting before the sheikh listening to a *hadīth* that he is relating, you are looking here and there and are easily distracted. Like this, some people go to the temple and spend their time looking at the clothes others are wearing. They go with one purpose, but having arrived they look at these other things. "What color shirt is he wearing today? What kind of shoes is she wearing? What jewels are they wearing?" People go to the mosque and the church but only pay attention to such things. They look to see if their relatives are there. Some think, "Who is here? What does that person have? What can we get from him? What help can he give me?"

This is how we are sitting in God's presence! Looking elsewhere! We are not looking for God when we are in the church, the mosque, the temple, or when we are in the presence of the sheikh. People sit in these places and look at the world. They focus on all the distractions. Even if such people are with the sheikh for a thousand years, this is all they will do. Such people do not really listen to what the sheikh says.

The sheikh is right here in front of you, talking and making an important point. He is looking right at you, but you are looking everywhere else. Your attention is elsewhere. Your mind is wandering.

When the sheikh is finished, he may ask, "Have you heard what I said?" But nothing will have penetrated. Each person was looking in a different direction and no one absorbed what was being said. Nothing entered their hearts.

If the sheikh asks, "Have you taken this in?" all are quiet because no one was paying attention. One person was looking at someone's sari. One was thinking about the world, his house, his life. Another person was looking up at the ceiling, watching a mouse crawl along the rafters. That person will answer, "Yes, yes, everything went in except the tail. The tail is still hanging out. I watched it very carefully. It came from the corner over there. . . ."

"What came?" the sheikh will ask in surprise.

"The mouse. It came from there, stood there, went there, and then went to that corner. It looked right at us and finally went into that hole. See there, the tail is still hanging out."

"So that is what you were looking at? None of what I said penetrated!"

"No," he will have to admit, very ashamed. The others in the room will also be quiet because they too were not paying attention.

What is the use of sitting in front of the sheikh in that state? You will never receive anything. Whether you are here for fifty years or five hundred years, it will not matter. It will be of no use.

Does the rain fall all the time? No. Therefore, when it does rain we must make use of it. We must plow and clear the land and sow what has to be sown. Only then can we receive the benefit of the rain. In the same way, will the sheikh be with you forever? No. Therefore, within the short time he is with you, you must cultivate so much.

The sheikh will not always be here talking to you. You must make a sincere effort and absorb the wisdom that rains now and cultivate your land. Now is the time that you can receive this wealth in your life. If you miss this opportunity, you cannot make up for it later. You will be the loser. You must clear the land and be ready to sow when the rain of grace falls. You must collect this *rahmat* and develop your soul. Only then will you receive the benefits.

It is in this state that you must sit before the sheikh, seeking and receiving what he gives. Otherwise you are only looking at various aspects of the world. Some people look at religions, some look at races and colors, some look at clothes, some look at their relations and connections. Some look for gold, property, houses, and possessions. Some proudly think, "Oh, I have learned everything." Some think, "I know how to recite the scriptures." There is no point in all this. You are only wasting your time. You must understand the value of each and every point the sheikh makes. You must absorb it fully, making use of every drop. You must open your heart so that the water of grace can flow into it. You must remain in that state and cultivate your land.

Instead, some of you are sleeping, some are talking, some are resting, some are dreaming, some are sitting here but wandering in your minds. You sit here and think, "Oh, I have to go shopping. I have to go to the bank. I have to buy shoes. I have to go to the store." You say, "Oh, we're bored and tired. We want to go sightseeing." When you think like this, the time is wasted. Even though you are here before the sheikh, your thoughts are elsewhere.

When a dog goes to a huge lake, it can only lap up small amounts, even though the lake is filled with so much water. Similarly, if you have this dog of desire within you, even if you are with the sheikh who pours so much into you, no matter how much love he gives or how much wisdom he pours out or how much compassion he shows, all you can do is lap up small amounts like the dog. Even if you are with a sheikh who gives you an ocean of water or an abundance of sweet tasting honey, you can only lick at it like a dog. You will still wish to wander about. Feces is like candy to a dog; no matter how much honey you offer it, it will always search for feces. Therefore, you have to train this dog and tie it up. Then you can absorb the sheikh's wisdom.

Although you are here with the sheikh, there are so many other things within you. You must try hard to receive every drop that comes from him. You will not be receiving this always; you have this opportunity only for a certain time. Within that allotted period, you must be able to cultivate your land and attain the benefits. To think that you can still receive this gift after the sheikh has died is not correct.

Use the fire while it is burning. If you try to create a flame from the cold wood after the fire has gone out, you will not succeed. You must switch on the light while the generator is still working. Once the motor has stopped, if you try to turn on the lamp, it will not light. Like that, while the sheikh is still in the world, you must learn wisdom from him. After he is gone, you will consider whatever the mind brings and whatever your thoughts bring as wisdom, but it will be just a dream of your mind. While you are with the sheikh, he can show you directly what is right and what is wrong. So, with each breath, in each moment, you must be with the sheikh. If you are always alert you will receive whatever you need. That will be your *hayāt*, your eternal life. That will be your wisdom.

You must make a sincere effort to do this. You must fully intend to receive whatever the sheikh gives and understand its weight. All the time you are wandering, you will not be able to cultivate that crop. You must correct yourself and take in every point. Every point is very heavy. Every word is heavy. Every look is heavy. Every thought is heavy. You must carefully receive them all and keep them in your heart. Then you will be able to benefit from these things. Think about this.

Do not be like the insects that live on the tree without realizing the value of its shade. Understand the value and weight of the words and actions of the sheikh, and accept whatever he gives you very carefully. Do not sit before him and look at the world or up at the sky. If you do, you will not receive anything. Reflect on this. You must know the type of life you need to nurture—the life of the soul. The wisdom you receive from the sheikh should be able to protect the life of your soul. Through that state of wisdom, you must be able to know and protect the purity of that *hayāt*. There are many deep meanings in this.

It is said that you must be with the sheikh for twelve years. What does this mean? After all, you can learn to recite the entire Qur'an in so many different ways in just two years. Yet you must be with the sheikh for twelve years. Why is this? What is it you have to learn? You must learn all that he has to give. What is that? His qualities, his actions, his conduct, his patience, his tolerance, his peacefulness, his compassion, his tranquillity, his serenity, his state of hunger, his state of vigilance, and the peace he has in the midst of joy or sorrow. You have to learn all this from the *gnāna* sheikh. It will take twelve years to learn his state of *sabūr, shukūr, tawakkul,* and *al-hamdu lillāh,* his peacefulness, and his tranquillity. If you learn all his qualities within those twelve years, then the fruit will ripen within you. Acquiring his qualities and his wisdom is the meditation you must perform during this time. This is how to understand what is within you. You must take the good as good and discard the wrong as wrong. That is how you must spend those twelve years.

You will not be doing this to receive *gnānam*, but rather to dispel *agnānam*, or ignorance, and to gather the qualities of *meignānam*, or true wisdom. You will be discarding the qualities of illusion and developing the qualities of God. As soon as these qualities grow within you, then a flower will bloom within your heart. As soon as that flower blossoms, its fragrance will emanate from every petal. When you reach maturity the flower will be in full bloom. That fullness and fragrance will appear, and you will be able to identify the flower. That will be God's flower. By its fragrance, it will be known that you are the child of God. Once that is known, you will know that taste of heaven, God's kingdom.

To learn this takes twelve years. By learning and imbibing all these qualities, this flower blossoms and its fragrance emanates from within. There is no other learning except this.

To do this you need wisdom. The wisdom that the sheikh gives you is the knife to cut away the thousands of animals in the jungle within your heart: the monkeys, the poisonous animals, the vengeful animals, the animals that eat one another, the animals that chase one another, the animals that separate one another. Wisdom is to cut away all these animals, to discard them one by one, to chase them away. Wisdom is there to cut and discard your arrogance, karma, maya, illusion, *tārahan, singhan, sūran,* lust, anger, miserliness, attachment, fanaticism, envy, intoxicants, desire, theft, murder, falsehood; the differences of the 'I' and 'you', 'mine', 'yours', property, bondage to relatives, the discriminations coming from differences of religion and philosophy; the emotions of jealousy, envy, treachery, deceit, hypocrisy, selfishness, considering one's own hunger more important than the hunger of others; aging, disease, death; the countless qualities of impatience, hastiness, passion, pride, envy, doubt; the glitters of illusion, mind, desire, and the monkey mind—all these have to be cut away and discarded.

You have to cut away all that is hell, chasing away the demons and ghosts within you. Discard all these evil things. To do this, you must receive that sword of wisdom from the sheikh. With that wisdom, you must battle each section in a different way. You must use the particular weapon necessary for each particular opponent. You need one weapon for ghosts, another for fairies, another for jinns, another for demons, another for the five elements, and still another for illusion and torpor. You need a different weapon for each of these things. It is only when you use all the necessary instruments that you can operate on the different illnesses and diseases which you have.

The *insān kāmil* gives you the wisdom to do all this—to dispel all your bad qualities and acquire and put into action his good qualities and the qualities and actions of God, thereby attaining perfection. It takes twelve years to teach you how to end your diseases and give you clarity and wisdom. When you have learned to end all your diseases, then you have received *gnānam.* Your heart becomes full, the flower blooms and the fragrance wafts forth. That fragrance is *gnānam.* When this occurs, then God is within you and the path is easy. This is wisdom.

Learning philosophies, the *purānas,* the Qur'an, or other scriptures can easily be accomplished in two years. But to establish this state within you correctly, to dispel all your bad qualities, and to receive the sheikh's qualities and actions takes twelve years. This is why it is said you must be with an *insān kāmil* for twelve years. You should understand this.

If you do not receive *hayāt,* eternal life, while you are alive and the sheikh is alive, you will not be able to receive it when the sheikh is gone. That cannot be done. What you receive at that time will be only a dream; you can see it while you sleep, but when you awaken it disappears. When the sheikh is alive, he is right there in front of you, whether you are awake or asleep. That is not a dream. He is there in front of you. You can talk to him. He can tell you what is right and wrong, what is good and bad, and you can understand. But if you let the allotted time pass, you will never be able to understand.

You must learn all this while both you and the sheikh are alive. Then you will remember it even when he is not there. If you can merge with him now, then this learning will remain with you. If you do not merge with him now, if you think you can accomplish this later, you are only deceiving yourself. Only if you mingle your qualities and your wisdom with the sheikh's will he be with you after he is gone. Then you will receive *hayāt*, eternal life. Each child should reflect on this and put it to use. Benefit from this. Try. *Āmin*.

Selecting a Disciple

My love you, my sisters, brothers, sons and daughters, my grandsons and granddaughters. When a father or a sheikh brings up his children, he looks at the state of each child and knows how each one will develop. The sheikh may have thousands or even millions of followers. When they first come to him, they are just ordinary people. Then from the hordes who come, a few are selected to become his disciples. Of this small group those who gain the most clarity become his children, his sons and daughters. This is the progression: first they are part of the general public, then they become disciples, and later they become his children.

In selecting disciples, the sheikh will note the exact behavior of each. He observes their intentions, their efforts, their certitude, their awareness, how they perform their duties, how they pray, and how they work. In every situation, he watches to see whether the disciple responds in an agitated or calm way. The sheikh observes every thought, every action, and every quality in each heart, their love, their sound, and their conduct.

Just as the magnet must be in the right position to attract iron, the disciple must also be in the right state for the sheikh to accept him and give him what he needs. Is he hasty? Does he have anger or resentment? Does he have jealousy or deceit? Is he lazy or is he clever? Does he have wisdom? Will his crop grow and provide benefit and peace to many or is it a poison that will destroy others when it matures? Or might it be turned into a tasty honey? The sheikh will watch every section in the development of that disciple. If he sees that his state will be good and that he will progress in the right way, the sheikh will make that disciple into his child and take that child into himself.

Next, he tries to give clarity to these children. Once a child has come out of the womb of the mother, you cannot send him back. You have to watch his development carefully. You must see whether the child has that intention for God, that seeking, that faith, and that awareness. Is the child absorbing what the father is teaching? Does he have a sense of duty? Has the proper connection between father and child been established? Only when there is a connection between the switch and the bulb will the light shine. If the connection is correct, you must next check to see whether the current is flowing through the wire correctly. Can it handle the full voltage and distribute it so that it can be used at certain points along the way, or will it be faulty? You have to check into this. Similarly, the sheikh will check to see whether this child can receive the current from the Source and direct it to the necessary points.

The sheikh has to continually test that child. He must test every quality of the child, prodding him to see his reaction. With each word and every action, he pricks the child to see how he will react. If the reaction is good, then he will take that child deeper into himself saying, "This child will turn out right."

This testing by the sheikh is similar to the way a certain type of wasp chooses its young. The wasp first builds a house of mud and then looks for a young one to place within it. The wasp does not lay eggs, instead it searches for a family. It searches for a young one that can take on its own qualities, conduct, and form. It tests to see which one is ready to follow its actions and learn its wisdom and patience.

There is a particular green worm that lives on the leaves. It forms a thread out of its own saliva, drops down on that thread, and hangs there. It is a beautiful insect. The wasp observes each worm that it finds on the leaves and pricks it with its stinger. If the worm trembles and becomes overly excited, the wasp decides, "This one is no good. It is hasty." So it leaves that worm and pricks another. If that one runs away in a hurry, this demonstrates that it does not have the quality to last until the end; when a small problem arises that worm will not be able to bear it and will run away. It will be uncontrollable in the mud house. So the wasp leaves that worm too and searches for yet another. Now when the next one is stung it just barely moves and then lies down again. "This one does not have sufficient effort in him. He is dull-witted and will not work hard no matter how much he is told. He will not turn out right,'' the wasp will conclude. So it looks still further. But the next worm shows no feeling and does not move at all even with continuous prodding. ''This one has no wisdom, intelligence, or feeling. Nothing will penetrate its ears. It is the worst kind of all,'' the wasp declares and that worm is also discarded.

Still the wasp continues searching. Eventually it finds a worm that moves just enough to avoid being stung. With each new sting, it adjusts itself, moving away slightly to avoid the pain and make itself comfortable. Quietly it shakes itself and moves away. ''Ah,'' the wasp says, ''This is the right one!'' Then the wasp takes that worm, places it inside the mud house, and seals the entrance. From that moment on, for the next forty to ninety days, the wasp flies around and around the sealed entrance repeating, ''Become like me. Become like me.'' Finally, the worm that was placed inside does become like the wasp outside. It takes on the shape of the wasp and slowly starts biting and scraping away at the mud wall. When the wasp hears this sound coming from inside, it breaks open the entrance. The worm which was placed within emerges in the exact form of the wasp that placed it there. Now, the new wasp will do the work of the old one.

Like this, when the sheikh selects a disciple from among a group of people, he prods, pricks, and analyzes. One by one he tests to see which one will progress. ''This man is an angry person. This one has resentment. This fellow is dull-witted and will be of no use. This one is a talker. This one has no feeling; he might listen but the words will not penetrate. This one will become caught up in whatever he is involved in at a particular moment and forget everything else. That one is hasty. This one wanders here and there and will not remain in one place to study." The sheikh watches all these qualities. Like the wasp, he continues to prod each disciple to see which one has the potential to improve. Then he takes those whom he thinks will improve and turns them into his children, his sons and daughters. In the same way that children in the world must be brought up by a father, the sheikh must bring up his children. Through his qualities and actions, he brings them up in wisdom.

Then once again he begins the process of pricking and prodding and testing. If ten children are selected he will determine which children can carry on his work and which children are suited for another kind of work. He decides and gives each one the appropriate duty. As a child progresses and reaches a state that promises growth, he takes that child inside himself, just as the wasp sealed the worm inside its house. The sheikh takes that soul, that child of truth, and seals him within the house of his heart. He places that child in his heart and repeats, "Become like me. Become like me." He goes on telling and teaching this to the child of his heart.

For twelve years the sheikh will continue teaching that child the words of God, His actions and conduct, His love, patience and compassion, His unity, peacefulness, tranquillity, and the awareness of treating other lives as one's own. He will show the child all the countless numbers of different qualities, animals, demons, and ghosts that exist inside the heart. He will explain about the angels, viruses, cells, insects, germs, water, blood, and fire; he will explain everything on the inside and outside. He will place these sons and daughters within himself and teach them. He will teach them about their physical form on the outside and about the purity of the soul and heart on the inside. He will show examples for the outside and the basic qualities for the inside. He will teach both the soul and the life within.

He will show you that whatever you see in the world outside, you must also learn to see inside, for it all exists within you. All the fire that you see in the world, you must recognize within yourself. You must identify all the animals, satans, snakes, insects, wasps, sun, moon, and stars, every being, all the four hundred trillion, ten thousand spiritual things, the mantras and ghosts and demons and all these astrologies—they are all contained within the five worlds inside you. There are no enemies on the outside. All your enemies are within. What you see outside is easy to understand, but have you understood the enemies within you? It is these enemies that you must learn to conquer.

Listen within. What is that sound? Ah, that is the sound of a snake. What is this sound? It is the sound of an elephant, the elephant of vanity. What is this sound? The sound of the force of the tiger. What is that sound? The mind—see how it jumps. What is this sound? A horse, running away. What is this sound? The bull that plows. What is this sound? A donkey. What sound is this? An eagle—see how it flies and watches below. What is this sound? A vulture searching for a corpse. What is this sound? The sound of a deer. What is this sound? A moose. What is this? A mountain goat. What is this? A python. What is this? A howling dog. What is this? A stork. What is this? A crow—it shouts about unity but is just making noise. That one is a monkey. All these ten-and-a-half million creations, countless numbers of creations are shouting inside. Where do all these sounds come from? They come from within you. The animals and other beings outside each have their own individual sounds, but within you are the sounds of all these inner creations. Within you is a vast world.

Man can make any sound; he uses a sound to lure something to him, and then he kills it. He makes the sound of a deer, and when the deer comes, he kills it for his own selfish reasons. He makes the sound of the elephant, and when the elephant comes he kills it. He makes the sound of a horse, and when it comes he catches it for himself. Man is the worst of all the animals. Everything he does is selfish. He has all the sounds within and he uses them for selfish gains. The other creations do not have that ability.

Man must destroy these sounds. He must rid himself of the sounds by which he lures these beings. He must try to make the enemies within peaceful. Each one will do its duty if properly trained. Do not destroy these lives within, but do not allow them to destroy and enslave you. You can control one with another. With fire you can control many beings, but fire itself can be controlled by water and by air. Air can be controlled by rain. Water can be controlled by ditches, by mountains, and stones. You can use one element to control another. Earth, fire, water, air, ether: if you can control these five you can control all the world, for the winds, sounds, and everything are all contained within these elements.

The father reveals all this to the child. He keeps the child within himself, raises him, and shows him all these examples. When the child is trained correctly on the inside, he will see no hostility or enmity on the outside. If he can control all the beings inside himself and show them wisdom and love, they will serve him on the outside, according to his command.

The sheikh will demonstrate all this and bring up that child placed within himself. He will raise that physical form on the outside and place the soul of that child inside to nurture it within himself. He will try to change that child into his own form and give him his own qualities, just as the wasp transformed the worm. He will rear the child with his wisdom and his qualities. Once his child acquires all the qualities of the sheikh, then he will hand the child over to God. From then on he is God's child and must learn from within God. The sheikh places the child within God and the child learns from God, from within. The sheikh turns his child into God's child.

This is how the sheikh brings a child from one step to the next. First he selects the child, then he raises him in his own form with his own qualities. The sheikh teaches the child to acquire God's qualities and finally hands him over to be brought up by God. At this point the sheikh will say, "Now You, O God, must protect this child. He is Your property."

This is the method of the sheikh as he prods, tests, and selects stage by stage, finally transforming the child into God's child. He keeps testing in order to select those few children. If the child jumps or is hasty, he passes that child by, saying, "Oh, this one is dangerous, this one has no control, this one might kill someone, this one might become an enemy, this one might sin against another life." He will leave the ones with these qualities behind and continue on his way.

This is how the true sheikh selects, tests, and teaches. There is so much testing to be done. He will pierce them with love, with wisdom, with his qualities and actions. Everywhere, in every section, he will prod and test his children to see their reactions. We must reflect upon this.

The ones who remain with the sheikh and are quiet and obedient will be selected, raised, and trained by the sheikh. You must understand this, children. You must have this effort, this intention, this awareness, and this feeling. When the sheikh sees these qualities in a child, he will teach that child on both the outside and the inside at the same time. On the outside he will teach your mind, and on the inside he will teach your soul and your wisdom. You must think about this. My love you, my daughters and sons. You must think about this.

Cutting the Gem

DISCIPLE: Every time I feel like I'm going on the right path, it seems that I am always bowled over by grief or sadness. It seems that I am going along okay and then everything explodes.

HIS HOLINESS: Somewhere there is a leak; the water is running out of the pond. There is a leak in the vessel in which you are preserving the water, and it is pouring out. To save the water you must stop that leak.

DISCIPLE: I can't seem to stop it through any outer effort. How can I control it from inside?

HIS HOLINESS: The water is inside. It is not on the outside. The water is within the pond, and the leak is in the supporting wall that surrounds the pond. That is the cause. If it is not repaired, it will break the mind. It will break the life. There is a leak in faith, a leak in *īmān*.

39

DISCIPLE: That is the reason I came to be with the sheikh.

HIS HOLINESS: All right, then control it.

DISCIPLE: Do you have a pill or something I could swallow?

HIS HOLINESS: Every day I give you such a pill, but you must swallow it correctly.

If whiskers grow on your face, you need a barber to shave them. Likewise, if hair grows inside, you need wisdom to shave it. The hair on the outside must be shaved with a very sharp razor. If you sit still, the barber can shave you properly, but if you continually fidget you will be cut. You cannot blame the barber or the razor. The razor's nature is to be sharp, so you cannot blame it. Neither can you blame the barber, for he is doing his job. The person who sits must sit correctly and be careful.

It is like that. Just as you shave your face to make it beautiful, the hair that grows in this mind has to be shaved to make it beautiful. To do so, your faith, certitude, and determination must be strong. Wisdom is very sharp, and you must be very careful when you shave with it. You must have that focus. There must be that point of truth to shave the mind. There should be no doubt, just truth. The hand of truth must hold this knife of wisdom.

Without this certitude, if you shift from side to side, no matter how clear the truth is or how sharp the wisdom is, you will be cut. The fault is not with the truth. The knife of wisdom has a natural sharpness; if your hand trembles that knife may cut you. If the angle changes, it may cut you. So the one who sits must sit correctly. Then the one who shaves can do his work. Wisdom can do its work and make the mind beautiful.

You must sit correctly with that strength. Then the sheikh will sharpen the knife for you. That sharp knife of wisdom will make your mind and heart beautiful. However, if the certitude with which you sit is not strong, you might be cut. This is the sorrow. This is the fault that you have. This is the reason each person experiences sorrow—the way he sits is not correct. My love you. Strengthen that. That is the leak in your life.

Take God's section within you. When you go to bathe, do not carry the fire of the world, the sins of the world, or the mind along with you. That fire will be doused by the water, and you will be sad because what you brought was destroyed. Fire cannot last in water. You must use wisdom.

DISCIPLE: Last night I had a dream about a house burning down.

HIS HOLINESS: Do not take that fire and keep it inside the cage of this body. It will burn down this house. That is not good. When you set out to clear yourself do not use fire to help you. Do not take the world or your karma along with you. These are the fires of sin, karma, and hunger. Do not take these with you.

My love you. You must think. The world is the fire that causes suffering to man; it destroys man. All his thoughts are fires. His intentions, desires, his attachment to relationships and bloodties; differences of religion, languages, and colors; love, hunger, old age, disease, death, selfishness, doubt, anger, resentment, and hastiness are all fires. Hypocrisy, ignorance, talking without wisdom, desire for earth, sex, and gold are all fires. There are countless numbers of fires which we are feeding within us. Every day man is being scorched by these flames. There is not a day when he is not being burned by one of these. Attachment to property, livestock, children, house, and wife; arrogance, karma, illusion; *tārahan, singhan, sūran;* lust, anger, miserliness, fanaticism, envy, intoxicants, theft, murder, falsehood—all these are fires in man's life. They are the fires of sin. Every second man is being burned; he is living in this fire. Man's plight is worse than that of the animals. This is hell! Man is suffering in this hell. He shouts, he cries, and then he smiles. One moment he says, "Oh, this is nice and cool," and the next moment he cries, "Oh, this is unbearable!" This is what man has found in life.

The way a true sheikh makes us suffer is not meant to harm us. He makes us suffer to rid us of our bad qualities, to kill the qualities that are feeding these fires. He is not trying to murder you. But when he cuts each one of your bad qualities, you cry, "*Aiyō,* he is cutting my attachment. *Aiyō,* my love! *Aiyō,* my mother, my mother! *Aiyō,* my grandfather!" You complain as each attachment is being cut. You shout, "*Aiyō,* my boyfriend is going! My schoolteacher! My house!" It hurts as he cuts them, one by one. You become angry, you feel resentment, you feel hatred, your mind becomes disturbed, and doubt creeps in. This is what happens when the good sheikh douses these fires one by one. He is not trying to harm you. He is trying to cut your evil qualities. This is his work; he is doing this so that you can have peace.

You are burning in this fire! You think it is good to be in this fire, but it is drinking your blood. You do not understand; this is your ignorance. Use your wisdom to look within. The good sheikh cuts these four hundred trillion, ten thousand spiritual ghosts, spiritual fires, jinns, fairies, heavenly beings, demons, elements, four-legged animals, monkeys, donkeys, rats, peacocks, crows, pigs, dogs, foxes, crocodiles, lizards, chameleons, and reptiles away from you. They all have a hold on you.

My child, consider the armadillo. When an armadillo grabs onto the trunk of an elephant, the elephant cannot breathe. It trumpets and shouts. A foolish elephant will strike its trunk against a tree or a rock in an attempt to free itself, but the more the elephant beats the armadillo, the harder it tightens its hold. It grabs on harder and harder with its claws. The armadillo is very strong, and its arrogant grab hurts.

Now, a wise elephant will start running as soon as the armadillo catches hold. The wise elephant knows there is only one way to free himself. He will run to a pond and stick his trunk into the water. He will keep his trunk submerged so that the armadillo cannot breathe. Now it is the armadillo who has to escape. It will release its hold and quickly run away. Then the elephant will walk away thinking, "Ah, I have escaped!" That is the action of a wise elephant.

Like that, once you know what is grabbing you, submerge it in wisdom, in God, and in truth. Then the evil qualities will leave you and run away. If you keep beating them against earth, fire, water, and illusion, they will hold onto you even more tightly. The more you strike them against attachment, desire, and bloodties, the firmer they will grab onto you. If you continue to beat them against fanaticism, color, and race, they will hold fast. That is not the solution. Submerge yourself in truth, wisdom, and patience. Reach into these good qualities; then the evil qualities will leave you of their own accord. This is how you must escape. This is how to use your wisdom. This is what a good, true *gnāna* sheikh, a true man, will do.

As he cuts away each section, your mind will feel pained; your attachments and intellect will experience pain and sorrow. All such thoughts will feel hurt. A good sheikh has to cut all this. You must think, "If he makes me suffer, it is only to kill the bad qualities within me and to extinguish this fire. That is why he is doing this." Think of it in this way. Remember that he is extinguishing the fire of karma which is scorching you and causing you to suffer. He is cutting the fire of hunger, the fire of doubt, and the fire of arrogance within you. He is cutting the karma of the five elements within you.

You are enticed by this illusion; you are steeped in it. The sheikh is cutting this. He is cutting the fire of desire. He is cutting your connection to the seventy thousand battalions of monkeys within you. He is cutting the connection to the body, to lust, to your anger, jealousy, envy, and resentment. He is cutting each and every connection. You become involved in things without looking, thinking, or realizing. The sheikh is cutting that tendency. He is cutting such thoughts and the differences of the 'I' and 'you'. As he severs each section it hurts. But wisdom and truth do not experience any pain. It is your mind that experiences pain. Your thoughts feel pain. Desire knows this pain. Your blood attachments suffer this pain. Each time they are cut it hurts, and because of this you find fault with the *insān kāmil*, the true human being.

You must realize that the sheikh's work is to cut these things. He is not doing this for any selfish reason. He is an instrument and you are the gem in his hands. He is cutting you to bring out the original light of the stone. You are a precious gem that came into his hands. He must make that stone valuable and then place it in the treasury. It is in his hands, so he has to do that work. He does not benefit. He has nothing to gain. He makes you valuable and places you where you belong, in the treasury of God's kingdom. When you reach that place, when you attain that clarity, you will appreciate the value of his work. But until such time you will experience pain. The gem feels the pain as it is being cut and faceted, but if this is done in just the right way, later you will realize the great value of that work.

Gurus may give you a mantra and charge you two hundred and fifty dollars. They take your money and say, "All right, stay as you are. Remain the uncut stone that you are," and they leave. The work of a true man is different. There will be pain. It is like an abscess that must be cut so that the pus can be drained. When the abscess is opened, you will experience pain. You should not complain saying, "Oh, he is cutting it open!" He has to lance the infection to drain the pus. You will feel relief when this is done. Whatever the disease, it must be healed. Sores, abscesses, and infections have to be lanced. That is the work of a good sheikh. If each point that hurts is removed, then you will find comfort.

To be cut like this, you have to be with the sheikh for twelve years. It is not a small matter. It is not just a small fire. The fire is burning from the roots right to the top of the tree. The sheikh has to keep cutting away at these qualities of fire, one by one. This takes time. You need twelve years to accomplish this. It is of no use to merely be in his presence. You have to understand, bear up, and surrender. You must say, "Make me well," and offer yourself to be cut. You must have that faith and certitude. You must say, "It is not difficult to endure the heat of this pain. I must get rid of my disease." You must offer yourself with that certitude and determination.

This is the work of *insān kāmil*. It will cause pain, but you must endure. You have to reflect, realize, understand, and bear it up. To do this, you need peacefulness, patience, contentment, and absolute trust. You can avoid feeling this pain only if you have these qualities. You must think, "I have this disease, and now it is being treated. This is why I am feeling pain. But this must be done for me to get well. I have to be cured of this disease." Then bear it up. If that thought and certitude come within you, the pain will not disturb you, and you will become clear.

There are four hundred trillion, ten thousand diseases. Your thoughts and the fires created by these thoughts must all be cut. This is why you have to stay with a true man for twelve years. However, you must be a child who can bear this pain. You must realize, "This is my disease he is curing. My father is curing me." You must have faith. You must realize, "These fires are burning, and he is healing the wounds within me." If you can bear it with that patience, with that thought, and with that wisdom, it will be easy. Then you will not feel any pain, and one by one you will be rid of your ailments. Point by point you will rid yourself of these bad qualities. Section by section your karma will be cut off. One by one your sins will be cut away. One by one your doubts will be severed. One by one your desires will be cut. One by one all these connections will be cut. Then you will have freedom. You will have peace.

The work of a good sheikh is to rid you of your evil qualities. If these are disposed of, then God's power will come. Then you will be a gem placed in the crown of God, in His kingdom. You will be placed in that treasury. Such is the work of an *insān kāmil,* a true human being.

You must think of this and persevere. He is cutting

away your thoughts. You think they are something very precious, so when he cuts them it hurts you. Instead, you must think, "This is something bad that he is cutting away." If you think like that, with patience, then you can endure the pain. Then he will remove the infection, this fire, and you will be comforted. However, if any shred of doubt is present while the sheikh is cutting, that doubt will become a cancer. You must remove all such thoughts. Then you and the sheikh will become one. Then there will be only one.

Each child must think about this. This is not a business. Is there any profit in cutting off a section of one's own body? Your body is the sheikh's body. Your illness is his illness. Your fire is his fire. This is what he is cutting. Two do not exist. The disease is within him, so he is cutting it. You should not see it as two. Your disease and suffering are his, so he is cutting himself. There is no duality. Do not think you are separate. This disease has come within his own body; he is cutting his own body. That is the work of a good sheikh. Because you are within him, you too will feel that pain. Because you have that disease, you will feel the pain. You must think about this.

So much cutting has to be done. When ignorance is cut, it hurts. The tears we shed from the eyes are seen by the world, but no one sees the crying on the inside. What comes from the eyes is water and any man can see those tears. But when you cry inside, it is blood that flows. There are ghosts within that drink your blood. Outside we may see just a small wound, but inside they are drinking the blood. God looks at the blood that is being shed inside, and He cries for that. Truth, God, and the good sheikh see the blood that is shed inside, and they cry. Their work is to cut that section. We have to stop the tears that shed blood. Each child must think about this.

DISCIPLE: How did we get so lucky to be here?

HIS HOLINESS: You must have had a previous connection to God, and that is what brought you here. Just as the seed has a connection to the earth, you have that connection to God, and that is growing within God. Just as a seed sprouts within the earth, you have a point within God. You must have had some truth within you, and that is growing. Some good that you did earlier or recently, or in the womb, or somewhere, some good that you have done has come back. A dot, an atom, a particle has come. There was a depression in the earth and so it was filled with water.

My love you, my child. May God help you.

The Father's Love

My children, there is something each one of you must think about. There should be no doubt in your hearts. You should not have arrogance, doubt, or anger. The father's love, the father's property, and the father's words are common to all. They are given equally to all the children, but because of your own faults you might be unable to receive what he gives.

The father has two breasts. With one he gives the milk of wisdom and with the other he gives you love. With the milk of wisdom he cares for you and dispels your hunger, illnesses, and old age. How you drink that milk, how you suckle the breast, and how you embrace your father determines whether the hunger of your worldly body and the hunger of your soul will be appeased. It all depends upon your own effort.

Whoever is hungry must search for and come to the place where his hunger can be satisfied. The nipple is the same for everyone; it is not small for one and large for another. Each breast has three openings. The amount you receive depends upon the manner in which you draw from it. If you do not receive enough, perhaps the fault is in your concentration or effort. If you are distracted, looking here and there while trying to nurse, you will not be able to finish within the allotted time. You should not be jealous and think, ''That person is drinking, this person is drinking. She is doing well, but I am unable to get the milk I need.'' Instead, you should embrace the father and appease your hunger.

Just as an infant drinks the milk gently without hurting either the mother or himself, you must have the same gentleness and love when you draw milk from your father. If you draw gently, the milk will flow. But some people try to bite and as a result draw blood rather than milk. Others just open their mouths and expect the milk to flow in, but it does not come. You must hold the breast and position your mouth in the proper way. You must embrace your father and drink the milk with proper love. Only then will the hunger of both your body and your soul be satisfied.

Your effort, your concentration, and your love will determine your success. It is your responsibility to draw the milk of love, the milk of wisdom, and the milk that appeases your hunger in this world. If this is not done correctly, it is not the father's fault. It is you who are at fault.

It is your own faults that torture you. You have arrogance and differences. Because one child is careful and drinks correctly, she may be developing and growing. She came with a purpose, she did what she came for, and she is growing. But some of you waste your time with arrogance, differences, doubt, and the ego of the 'I'. Therefore, you are unable to drink the milk of wisdom that is necessary to make your life and wisdom grow.

Understand first that your father has two breasts and two nipples which provide equally for all. Do not think, "That person is growing and progressing well. I am not progressing. I don't have a place here." If you think that you do not belong here, it is because you do not have the ability to make room for yourself or to make yourself fit in. You are distracted by looking at others, and you are not taking enough care. If you make an effort to drink in the proper way, you can progress. Think about this.

Your doubts come from your own attitudes of discrimination. As a result, the hunger of your soul is not appeased; the hunger of the world and the hunger of your life are not appeased. Whose fault is this? It is each one's own fault.

Understand you are all children born to the same father. You are all brothers and sisters, yet you say each child is different. You say, "You are different. I am different. I have no place here. They have no love for me." The reason for this is that *you* have not embraced your brothers and sisters. Your heart should go and embrace them. You must hold them with your love.

Consider the example of a tree. A tree grows very high, and although it is only a single tree, it produces so many delicious fruits. You must examine its fruits and select one that has good color and taste. Then you must eat that fruit. Do not stand on the ground and try to knock down a fruit by throwing stones. You might miss, and even if you do hit one, it will be damaged when it falls. You must try to climb that tree. How should you proceed? First you must look carefully to see whether there are any footholds such as broken branches upon which you can climb. See if there are any thorns to be avoided. Assess the tree, then put your hands around it, and climb. Then you can reach the fruits and eat.

The father has the fruit. Just as you have to first embrace the tree to reach the fruit, your love must first embrace the father. Then with that love you should climb up. Only if you climb in this way can you obtain the fruit. If you do not embrace with love, if you do not put your hands around the tree and climb with love, the tree will remain silent and the fruits will remain out of reach.

Similarly, you must also embrace your brothers and sisters with your love. If you embrace each other with the hands of love and then climb, you can eat those beautiful, undamaged fruits. But if you remain on the ground and throw stones, the fruits will be damaged and you will never find unity in life. Your doubts will increase and no fruits will ripen. Neither unity, love, nor joy will develop within you. You will not be able to progress. This is what you will experience in your life if you do not show love. If you do not develop love in your heart and become humble, if you do not open your heart, then other hearts will not come to embrace you. But if you keep an open heart, others will come to you with open hearts.

Each of you must purify your own heart. You must

show your love. You must show unity and equality. If you show compassion and justice, you will progress and become exalted. But if you have doubt in your mind and the arrogance of the 'I', such qualities will cause you to suffer and may eventually kill you. This doubt and arrogance will separate you from goodness and from God. It will separate you from truth, unity, and compassion. It will separate you from Allah. Your life will be separated from wisdom, and you will be separated from that melting, dissolving love. You will be separated from good wealth and receive instead the wealth of fire, which is deceit, treachery, anger, hastiness, impatience, pride, falsehood, theft, murder, and sin. These will cling to you and become a part of you. Both while you are alive and after you have died, you will be living in hell. You yourself will have created this state.

God is love. Charity is great. If you open your heart and show God's love and His compassionate qualities, then grace, wealth, and tender love will develop within your heart. His *rahmat,* His beauty, and His light will develop in your heart. Fruits which never perish and unending treasures will appear there. God's grace and treasures will resplend there. Unity and the understanding that all lives are like your own life will develop in that open heart. You must think about this.

However, if you close your heart, when the One with love comes and knocks, He will say, "Oh, this is closed," and He will go away. Treasures will come and say, "Oh, this house is closed. It is a dark house," and they will leave. God's grace will come and say, "Oh, this house is ruined," and will leave. Even if someone comes with great love, he will see that this house is locked and in ruins, and he will leave. If you lock your heart, nothing can enter. Therefore, you must open your heart and keep it open. Only then can you receive the benefit. Only then can you receive truth and peace and find tranquillity in your life. You must think about this.

If you do not reflect upon this, your doubts, arrogance, and jealousy will consume you and separate you from God, truth, and wisdom. You will be separated from a life of exaltedness, and you will bring degradation to your life. You need to understand this eternal love. You need to know how much taste there is within the milk you take from your father. With unity, you must imbibe this milk.

My precious jeweled lights of my eyes, in the past, cars had rubber horns which you had to squeeze to make a sound. The air on the inside would go out and the air outside would come in, creating a sound. Just as air escapes when the horn is pressed and new air enters from the outside, if you draw upon the nipple with good conduct, with prayer, love, and purity of heart, that nipple will remove what is bad and fill you with the good milk. You must drink from that breast with love. If you drink the milk properly, behave in the correct way, and embrace the father, you will receive all the milk you need. Only then will your karma, your sins, and the doubts which you have accumulated be taken away.

The children who drink carefully will progress. But a child who does not drink with care will not receive enough nourishment and there will be deficiencies in the spiritual life of that child. Such a child will feel discriminated against and suffer from doubts. He will say, "That child is being treated better than I am." But the fault is within himself. It is his own behavior, his own qualities, and the state of his heart which causes this.

You must know how to embrace your father and drink his milk in the correct way. You must know how to grow and achieve unity. You must know clearly how to accomplish this. Think about this and understand how to be nurtured by your father, how to behave with your brothers and sisters, and how to embrace the truth and end your suffering. Only then will you attain peace and tranquillity in your life. Only then will you find victory in your life in this world and in the life of your soul. You will find comfort and joy in this world and the next. In both joy and sorrow you will have peace. You will find peace with your sisters and brothers, and you will achieve victory in the life of this world and the next. Then you will receive God's *rahmat,* His benevolence. Do you understand? You must think about this and develop the state in which you can conduct yourself in this manner. If this state is achieved, you will not be angry or find fault with one another, you will not deceive one another, and you will not attack one another.

My children, the fragrance of the flower does not exist separately outside the flower, but is contained within. When the flower opens, the fragrance is revealed. If the flower does not open, the fragrance is not known. We can see this, can we not? Before the flower blossoms can you appreciate its color? No. Can you smell the fragrance of the flower when it is closed? No.

Like that, if your heart is closed, it will never be beautiful. If your heart is shut, neither the beauty nor the fragrance will be revealed. Only when the flower blossoms does the fragrance emanate. If your heart is constricted, the bliss and beauty will not be experienced. Only when your heart blooms will the fragrance of grace, the fragrance of wisdom, the fragrance of the soul, and the fragrance of Allah's *rahmat* come forth. It is all there within your heart, and when it blooms, its beauty, fragrance, and beautiful quality will be revealed.

If the heart is open, all those who love this fragrance and who can appreciate its scent will draw near that heart and say, "Oh, this is beautiful. It has a wonderful fragrance." Those with wisdom will come and appreciate you. Those who can experience this fragrance will realize your beauty. Only when your heart has bloomed will others love you and come in search of that flower of the heart. They will smell that fragrance and recognize the love and beauty in your heart.

You must keep the flower of your heart safe. That is a flower garden. You must not think that this garden is somewhere outside of you. Some say that heaven is filled with beautiful springs, beautiful houses, and gardens. But there is no place called heaven outside you. It is within. All those houses, gardens, fruits and flowers, all the seventy thousand fragrances of flowers and the seventy thousand tastes of the fruits are within your heart. The river of milk, the river of honey, and the river of ambrosia are all within your heart. This is the pure house. The heart is your kingdom of heaven, your Father's kingdom. This is your prayer mat, your place of worship. This is the flower garden of your life. Your qualities are the flowers and your actions are the fruits of that garden. Your duty, your love, and your loving qualities are the seventy thousand tastes in that fruit. The duties and actions that you do for God here in the world will become the houris that serve you there. Your prayers will become the heavenly beings and angels who serve you there. The benefits you earn and what you seek in this world will be the house created for you there. Depending on the work that you perform here, the wealth will be given to you there—the wealth of grace, the wealth of the next world, the wealth of '*ilm,* and the wealth of *rahmat.* According to how you pray, you will attain peace and tranquillity. According to how you perform your work, you will receive the garden of fruits, the kingdom of God, and the precious gems; each good thought will be a gem inside. Your open heart, your open *qalb,* your open actions, and the beauty that develops within your heart will be your beauty and wealth in the next world. They will be your jewels in *ākhir.*

All that you receive in the next world will have already been created in your heart. That is your heaven. Whatever is within your heart will be given to you there in the next world. You will draw your happiness from within this flower garden, this orchard of fruits, this river of milk, this river of honey and grace. Each fruit that ripens there depends on the prayers, actions, and good qualities that you develop. That fruit is imperishable and its beauty undiminishing.

That honey is here, that grace is here, and that milk of love is here. The milk of grace which melts and softens the heart is here in your heart. The house that you prepare here in your heart will be the heaven you will receive later. You take the deed of ownership with you. If you have not prepared this house, this orchard, and this flower garden here, if you have not developed that taste, that beauty, and your duty in this birth, it will be the cause of your difficulty in the hereafter.

Allah's *ka'bah,* His place of worship, is here within the heart. His judgment and His kingdom are here within the heart. You must manage that pure kingdom in the correct way. Allah's kingdom must be managed by Allah. We must imbibe within ourselves His qualities, His blessing, His actions, His intentions, His patience known as *sabūr,* His contentment known as *shukūr,* His *tawakkul* or trust, His three thousand gracious qualities, and His ninety-nine *wilāyats* or powers. Each one of us must search for His *wilāyats* within ourselves. If we can find this beauty, this peace and joy within, then we will reach the state of a true believer, a *mu'min.* A *mu'min* is one who has received the light of Allah and has no blemishes, faults, differences, or discriminations. Such a one has attained peace within himself and has found peace in all lives. He gives peace and love to all and embraces all lives, relieving their sorrows and suffering.

If you do not aspire toward this compassion and love, if you do not build this house within your heart, if you do not cultivate this orchard of fruits, if you do not discover the river of milk, the river of honey, the river of grace, the only river which can quench your thirst, if you do not find the happiness contained within your heart, if you do not act with His qualities and with the peace, tranquillity, and unity which are the wealth of Allah, if you do not see all lives as your own and serve them, if you do not perform all these services—then you will be in a state of hell. You will have a life devoid of peace. The house you build will be a house of hell.

Hell is the evil desires of the world, the mantras, magics, and tricks of illusion known as *indira jālam.* Hell is arrogance, karma, treachery, deceit, jealousy, and anger. Hell is dwelling in the differences between 'I' and 'you'. Hell is discrimination, hypocrisy, falsehood, vengeance, deception, pride, desiring praise, spreading lies, cursing, and backbiting. As long as you have these qualities you are living in a house of hell during this life itself. When you die and are in the grave you will also be in a house of hell. You will have to suffer in this world, in your grave, and in the next world.

If you build a house of hell in this world, you will burn in the fire in the pits of hell. In this world itself you will undergo suffering. You cry and you laugh; one moment you are happy and the next moment you are sad—that is your house of hell which you have built by your own bad thoughts and actions. Once you have constructed this house you will suffer in hell in both this world and the next. This is the state which you will attain in both your heart and your life.

It is easy to talk about this, but you must truly open your heart, realize, and understand the truth. There is no use in mere talking. Open your heart, analyze it, and then prepare that beautiful house. With wisdom you must analyze and cultivate the farm within. You must build your own beautiful house, the house of grace. You must build a house of *rahmat* and collect the wealth of that *rahmat*. You must gather the treasures of the three worlds and build a house for this world, for the world of the soul, and for the next world. If you gather the *mubārakāt*— the triple blessings of the house of Allah's *qudrat,* Allah's wealth, and Allah's *rahmat*—then you will always have this undiminishing treasure. You will not be reborn. You will attain that undiminishing grace and joy without sorrow. You will have a long life without sadness or suffering. You will be eternally joined with Allah living in His house. Your house will be your Father's house. That is the *firdaus* of life. That is paradise. To reach that state, you must search for the divine qualities and the true knowledge known as *'ilm.* You can receive these treasures from a father who has wisdom and *'ilm.* You can receive these treasures and the exaltedness of your life from such a father.

My precious jeweled lights of my eyes, children born to me, you must think about the goal of your efforts and your search. You must reflect upon what these treasures are. If you pour one drop of water onto the ground, it will moisten the ground. As the water continues to drip, it will begin to loosen the soil. Then if you dig deeply, you will find enough water to quench the thirst of many. Likewise, if you begin by doing one duty for Allah, and then continue to perform your duty in an effort to reach that One spring, many springs will open within you. His grace will gush forth.

The prayers you perform, the duties you do, the charity and love you give, the unity you have, and the lessons you learn are all equal to just one drop. But if you use that one drop and continue to do your duty and keep digging within, then the spring of Allah's grace and His qualities will flow in abundance. As soon as you pour that one drop, you will receive so much. If you give Allah just one word, you will be able to hear so many of Allah's words of grace. All that you hear will be a wealth that belongs to you. If you make the effort and search for Allah with the amount you have now, whatever its limits may be, and if you continue to search with determination, you will receive so much from Allah. You will receive what rightfully belongs to you. You will attain peace and be relieved of your fatigue. Then with this abundant water of grace, you can give peace to others and relieve them of their fatigue. The spring of grace, the spring of light, and the spring of knowledge will all flow in abundance, and you will be able to satisfy and give peace to all.

Even though each effort may equal just one drop,

if you constantly search with that one-pointedness, it will act like the steady dripping which loosens the soil and allows you to dig deeper. This search is your birthright. You have to try. You have to make the effort. Within that effort is love, and within that love the fruits of your effort will ripen. As you dig within that love there will be a melting and dissolving; many springs will open up within you, and you will experience Allah's wealth and peace. Then hunger and sin will end. All the karma, arrogance, and evils of the past and present will end. The hunger of the soul, the hunger of this world, and the hunger of the next world will be appeased.

But if you give just one drop and think, "I did this! I gave so much!" then there can be no benefit. God gives abundantly. He pours with plenitude. That is His treasure. He does not say, "I am doing this." You give only one tiny drop of prayer to Him. Even if you pray to Him with sincerity, it is only equal to one drop. If you search for Him earnestly, it still is not equal to even one drop of His love. You might do just a little and then say, "I have done so much," but He gives in abundance. You should think about how much He gives, how He causes things to increase and multiply.

You must forget the 'I'. In all your prayers you must surrender and give all responsibility to Allah. Whenever you do anything, say, *"Al-hamdu lillāh, all praise is to Allah."* When you walk, say, *"Al-hamdu lillāh."* Whatever you do, first give responsibility to God and then do it. If you perform your duty in the proper way, if you open that spring and attain

His *rahmat,* then you can give water to all people, to all lives. With that water you can feed those born with you and fill their hearts with His grace. Only then will you become God's child. You will live in God's house and He will live in your house. That is the house of *rahmatul-'ālamīn,* the house of the mercy and grace of all the universes. *Al-hamdu lillāh.*

Think about this. Open your hearts and cultivate this garden, this farm. Build this house within the heart. Establish the kingdom of Allah within your heart. Make an effort and work hard. Then you will receive His *rahmat.* Do not think about the various races, religions, and scriptures. You should only strive for Allah's treasure. To attain Allah's *rahmat,* a life of victory, and victory for your soul, drink the milk of the father. Through that you can find peace. This is what is contained within the heart of an *insān kāmil.* This is the heaven that you can find within yourself. This is the treasure.

As-salāmu 'alaikum wa rahmatullāhi wa bara-kātuhu kulluhu. May the peace of God and His beneficence be upon all of you. *Āmīn.*

According to how you listened to this *hadīth,* you will reap the benefit. This is the way to perform duty to Allah. You must try to receive this benefit. Allah is the Almighty One. He is the One worthy of all praise and praising. He is the One worthy of love and service. He is the One who belongs to love and to service. He is the form of compassion. May we be open to receive His treasures with melting and open hearts.

Children, my precious jeweled lights of my eyes,

all children who have love for Allah, wherever they may be, may Allah give you the treasures of the three worlds, the treasures of grace, the treasures of *'ilm,* the treasures of the soul, and the treasures of *ākhir.* May He give all these treasures in completeness.

May You give peace to the hearts of my children. May You help them find peace. *Āmīn. Yā Rabbal-'ālamīn.* So be it, O Lord of the universes. *As-salāmu 'alaikum wa rahmatullāhi wa barakātuhu kulluhu.* May the peace of God and His beneficence be upon all of you. *Āmīn.*

The Difficult Path

A guru (a false sheikh) will give you a room in hell while he becomes a pillar of hell. You will be the inhabitants of hell and he a pillar of hell. He conducts his life with the title of guru and receives praise, fame, a name, and plenty of good food. This is the self-business he performs.

There may be many gurus like this in the world, but it is difficult to find a *gnāna* sheikh, a *gnāna* guru. To establish a connection with such a one is very difficult. To do this, your qualities and the sixty-four sexual arts and games must be cut away. The *gnāna* sheikh must cut away all the four hundred trillion, ten thousand 'spiritual' qualities. Whichever side you tend to stray toward will have to be cut. Whatever you bring, whatever you speak or sing, he will cut away. Whatever thoughts come to you and whatever you look at will be cut away. He will block all the scorched paths on which you are traveling. He will block all the paths of your desire. Therefore, it will be difficult. The *gnāna* sheikh will take you on his path. He will show you only one path and cut away all the others.

My children, you must think. Do not look at the world; look at yourself. Do not find fault with the world; look at yourself with wisdom. Do not be angry with the world; discover the faults you have within. Do not research into worldly life; your own life and a vast world are within you. Look within your body and see the faults it performs. Think about that and look.

Do not pay attention to the speech of the world. There is so much speech within you from the time you are born until the time you die. Do not read books about the world; read your own history within. You have the history of the four hundred trillion, ten thousand births. Look at that history book. This is the history which has a connection from *awwal* to *ākhir,* from the world of the soul to the hereafter. That history is not written down. It must be brought into focus by your wisdom; then all the letters can be seen. It is like invisible ink; you cannot see anything until the ink is heated, and then all the letters are revealed. The five elements of earth, fire, water, air, and ether are the letters written with this ink. Hold them before the heat of wisdom and look.

Under the light of the resplendence of Allah, you must hold this history in the heat of wisdom and look. Then you can read what is written. When you hold it this way, you will be able to see the past twenty million years of history. You will be able to see earth, fire, water, air, ether, and each form that has existed since the beginning of creation. Like this, there are so many things you must learn in life.

You say that you pray and worship, but you are doing what the world does. Look at what God does. See how He prays, how He proceeds, how He performs His duty, how He serves, how He is a slave, how He is a great one, how He is a small one, how He is a complete one, how He is a poor man, how He does not live in any particular place and yet is in every place. Understand all this history. Understand what prayer is, and understand what worship is.

In the light of Allah, in that resplendence, hold this book under the heat of wisdom and look. Look into your innermost heart, your *qalb*. When you examine your history in this way, you will understand what is good, what is evil, what is unjust, what is eating away at you, what is enslaving you, what is causing you to suffer, what is holding you, and what is killing you. Look at all these diseases. These are your illnesses.

You must study this history now, to rid yourself of these illnesses. Every second, every minute, the lessons you must learn are within. Do not waste your time looking outside at this and that. These paths are all diseases that will kill you. These are the diseases that will destroy you. These are the diseases that will induce torpor in you. This is why all these paths are blocked by a *gnāna* sheikh. Do not go on these paths.

Life is no more than waking up one moment and dying the next. Sometimes you are conscious, sometimes you are not. You are awake, then you fall asleep, then you awaken again. One moment you cry, one moment you laugh. You do all these things. Whatever you desire you try to carry with you, but when you can no longer bear it, you cry. Wherever you walk, whomever you follow, the mind will run away and desert you in the middle of your journey. Then you may be caught by the animals of the jungle. If you set out to sea, the mind may steer your boat for a while, but later it will leave you adrift and run away. You then become food for the sharks. Like this, all the paths prepared by your thoughts are diseases that will kill you.

You think, "There is light, there is *gnānam,* there is a guru, there is completeness, there is heaven, there is gold and silver, there is a palace," and you follow these thoughts. Such are the dreams that you see. They are illnesses. They will all desert you midway, leaving you subject to illusion, hell, currents, magnetism, desires, attachments, religions, race, satan, hell, worms, and insects. Your mind will lead you into all these predicaments and run away. Then you will suffer.

There are countless lessons within that you must learn. There are eighteen thousand worlds in *arwah, āwwal, dunyā,* and *ākhir* (the world of the soul, the beginning of creation, this physical world, and the hereafter). These are the lessons which you must study in your life. A *gnāna* sheikh will tell you to read the book within.

There are sixteen types of gurus, but only one point, one sheikh. If you find that *gnāna* sheikh, the world that you bring with you will be blocked. The sixty-four sexual arts, the races, religions, your desires, your attachments, everything will be blocked. An *insān kāmil* will show you only one

70

treasure and block all the others. He will show you only one soul, one life, and cut away all the other lives. Only one path will be open, the path which extends from the east to the west. Whatever you see in between will be closed to you. The sheikh will say, "Do not turn at this junction; it is blocked. Do not look at that intersection, another group is there. Go on the straight path!" Such is the difficulty undergone by a disciple with an *insān kāmil*. The difficulties arise from the difference between what you want and what he says. However, if you set out to do what he wants, putting aside all your desires, then you will be able to go with him.

Many may come to this true sheikh, but unable to bear this path, they run to the other gurus who let them do whatever they want. They all gather in the marketplace for business—for guru business, religious business, and caste business. They all come to this market saying, "We want to attain *gnānam,* we want to receive miracles and *siddhis,* we want to reach God, we want to find heaven." Because that type of guru is running a self-business, he will join with you and allow you to do as you please. If a dog eats feces and the guru is also willing to eat feces, then the relationship is good. If the guru wants milk, then he will keep a cow. Each thought you have that benefits him is acceptable. If you want to be a prostitute and he is a prostitute, then that is suitable. If you want to be a thief and he is a thief, then that is acceptable. If he has what you desire, then it is an agreeable relationship and you will remain with him. However, if he is a true sheikh, he will block all these sections, and you will find it difficult. To this you will say, "Oh he is a fool, a crazy man. He won't let me go to the market. He won't let me go here or there. What kind of fool is this man?" What the *gnāna* sheikh says may hurt you, but it is only your thoughts that will be hurt. All your desires and attachments will be hurt by what he says. Your mind and intellect will make you suffer, and because of this some disciples become angry and leave.

This is why you find very few people with the *gnāna* sheikh. He will not have many disciples, maybe one or two or three or four or maybe ten or twenty. Even twenty would be considered a large number. The followers of a *gnāna* sheikh will be the minority, not the majority. However, if he can find fifteen or twenty followers, they will be the leaders for the eighteen thousand worlds. They will have received the wealth of God and will rule the kingdom of this world and the kingdom of heaven, God's kingdom. They will be God's funny family, the ant family.

Only those who are bound by the sheikh's words and commands will reach that state. All the others run away. The others will gather in the marketplace, but as night falls each will return to his own home. Those who buy from here and there, who take this and that, cannot stay. Many people come to buy *siddhis* and whatever they desire and then leave. They take what they want and then return to the place of karma. This is what happens in the world. Only this one group will remain in that station with the sheikh. They will stay within that one point in the sheikh's innermost heart. They will stay within his wisdom and his love; they will stay within his compassion.

It is a difficult path to be with an *insān kāmil,* a difficult learning and a difficult research. This is the research of life which you must understand within yourselves. You must have absolute faith, certitude, and determination in the sheikh, in Allah, and in the messengers of God. You must have this *īmān.* If you have this absolute faith, certitude, and determination, you can proceed without going wrong. You can hold onto the sheikh's shirttails and progress. But if you take one of the other paths, if you break through one of these blockades and keep going, you will be lost. You will be destroyed on whatever path you take.

For the truth, all these paths will be blocked. It will seem very difficult, and you may feel sad. But when you cut away all these difficult sections, in the end you will find joy. If you cut away all that seems difficult to your mind, you will find joy. If you continue cutting these difficulties with certitude, day by day, you will grow into completeness, into plenitude. But if you run away saying, "This is difficult," that very quality which is causing the difficulty will become a disease which will kill you. It will consume you day by day and slowly kill you.

Understand that this is how it is. This is how the ant man speaks. This is his type of learning. For this reason you will find it difficult to be with the ant man. All your thoughts and intentions will bring difficulties. That is why this ant man society will not

73

grow large. It is a difficult path. People will come to learn wisdom, but later they will run away. They will say, "I came to find *siddhis* and occult miracles. I got what I wanted and left." Such is their suffering.

Knowing this, stay with certitude and determination. Like the cowboy who watches over a thousand grazing cattle, you can attain that perfect completeness which can control this inner world. You can receive that grace and have the power to rule all the eighteen thousand universes and control everything.

You must stay with determination, certitude, faith in Allah, faith in the sheikh, and faith in the *rasūls.* Strengthen that *īmān.* Go on that path. Change into his child. Then you will find victory. You will find completeness and plenitude. You will find peace, equality, and tranquillity in your life. You must understand this.

My love you, my children, my daughters, my sons. My love you, children of my heart, who are going on the true path. This is the truth. On the path of truth there are so many obstacles, but you must follow this path. Otherwise you will never find peace, and you will experience even greater difficulties because of this. The sheikh will also never find peace, because the work he came to do will not be completed. You must endure all this and remain with the sheikh. *Āmīn.* May God help us. *Āmīn.*

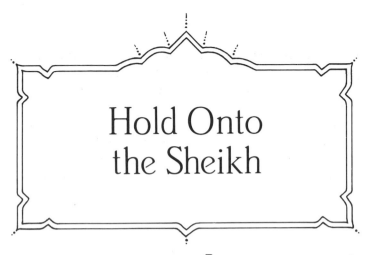

Hold Onto
the Sheikh

Bismillāhir-Rahmānir-Rahīm. In the name of Allah, Most Gracious, Most Merciful.

My precious children, jeweled lights of my eyes, there is a reason why the father and his children have gathered here together in one place. There is a connection between the father and his children. We must think about this.

Birds come from various lands and gather together in a fruit-laden tree, because they desire the fruit. Does that tree accept only one particular kind of bird? No, it is not exclusively for a myna bird, a parrot, or a dove; all God's creations are free to eat and enjoy those fruits. Each creation that comes in search of the tree can take according to its own tastes and needs. The tree and its fruits are common to all, showing no discrimination toward race, sect, or caste.

Truth is like that. Everyone can take from it, appease their hunger, and feel happy. Every living creature searches for that tree of truth. We have gathered here in search of a fruit and a taste that can give peace and tranquillity to the heart. We have gathered here in search of truth, wisdom, and God's love.

However, the taste of this fruit can only be known according to the qualities, thoughts, and desires of the one who tastes it. Many different birds of various colors come and sit upon the tree, but each experiences the taste of the fruit according to its own tongue. This has nothing to do with the tree or the fruit; they remain the same. The fruit always has the same smell, taste, and qualities. Only the bird that desires and truly savors the taste of this fruit alone will know its real taste.

In the same way, my children, we have all gathered here in search of God, the fruit of God, and the wisdom of God. But while we are trying to learn this wisdom, if we contaminate it with what we learned earlier, that is what we will taste. We will not experience the real taste of God. We will only discover our own qualities and see our own desires and attachments. In the very place we have come to learn wisdom, we will see our own suspicions and separations of race, sect, and color.

My children, we are all one family. We have gathered here to taste the same fruit. But we have various qualities, actions, desires, and attachments. In this state we are trying to taste the wisdom of God, yet we are only tasting our own qualities and actions. This is what causes difficulty. The fault is not with the source. We must reflect upon this. We must leave all our desires behind and taste with the tongue which tastes only that wisdom. Then can we truly relish that taste. Each one of us must reflect on this and understand.

DISCIPLE: The other day I was reading your discourse about "The Difficult Path" and I have been thinking how true that is.

HIS HOLINESS: You have been thinking, "How can I do this? I have a husband. If it is this difficult to live with the sheikh, should I go another way? I have a husband to look after."

True, it is difficult. It is very difficult to be with the sheikh. But if you leave the sheikh, with whom are you going to stay? Where will you find peace?

My child, although rain is generally considered beneficial, it can also cause destruction; it can bring both profit and loss. A beautiful house is supported by the earth, but later it could be destroyed by an earthquake. That is natural. Leaves will fall after a certain time. Trees will wither and die. The moon and the stars can be occluded by the sun. The sun brings the day but can be hidden by the night. Every creation can be subdued by another creation. Everything changes. From birth until the end, this is how it is.

A deer runs fearing that another animal will eat it. One runs and another pursues. Is there any peace? Each of God's creations will kill and eat another. None of His creations in the sea or on the earth live in peace or tranquillity, because each can be disturbed by another. What is there that lives peacefully?

Nothing. Even water cannot stay in one place. The waves form in the ocean, run to the shore, and then flow back to the sea. Nothing in the world of creation lives in peace, comfort, or tranquillity.

Do mind and desire have peace or tranquillity in the ocean of maya? Does the soul find peace? Does desire see an end to its wishes? Is there an end to your wanting new clothes? Does food or sleep give you peace? No. If you stay awake do you find peace? If you meditate do you attain the peace you need? Where can you find peace?

Within man there are three sections: the section of the body which contains mind and desire, the section of the soul, and the secrets of God. And there are three worlds: the world of this earth which is hell, the world of the soul, and the world of God. In which of these can you find peace or comfort? We can never find peace in life as long as we live in the ocean of maya. In order to find peace you must first examine yourself to find out what qualities you should keep and what you must discard.

Before you go on a journey, you always look in the mirror to check that everything is just right. Then you adjust your dress or hair according to what you see. On the journey of your soul, the sheikh is the mirror. Just as you beautify yourself in front of a mirror, you should stand before the sheikh in order to see what you must discard from within yourself. Standing before him, you must use your wisdom to clear your life, your mind, your ignorance, your qualities, and your actions. When you stand before the mirror of the sheikh, he will show you your self.

If you attempt to clear your faults, it is bound to be difficult. You may think, "If I stay with this mirror, life will be very difficult for me." But if you discard the mirror, all you do will be false. If you look in the mirror before going to a party and adjust whatever is necessary, you will look beautiful, but if you dress without using the mirror, others may laugh at you. If you throw the mirror away, saying, "Oh, this is a nuisance, I can't bother with it," you will experience even more suffering.

You cannot leave the sheikh just because it is difficult. The sheikh will clear your actions and conduct. He will show every defect only to give you beauty beyond beauty, action beyond action, patience beyond patience, equality beyond equality, peace beyond peace, wisdom beyond wisdom, truth beyond truth, *gnānam* beyond *gnānam,* grace beyond grace, and brightness beyond brightness. The mirror of the sheikh will show you that clarity which will exalt your life and increase your goodness. That is his work.

If you ask a dog to bathe, will it do so? Only if it is taught how. Otherwise, when it sees the water it will howl. If you try to force it into the water, it will bark and growl. Within you is the dog of desire and the monkey of the mind. If you try to wash them will they stand still? No. They will howl and jump and try to get away. They will try to bite and nip your arms and legs. You must not be afraid that the dog will bite you. Do not run away. Somehow or other, bathe that dog of desire. If necessary, tie it up or beat it. Pour water over its head, then brush and wash it.

In this way, my children, your mind and desire,

religions, philosophies, the world and illusions, the five elements, differences of colors and hues, arts and sciences, and even the food you eat will disturb you and try to make you run away. But you must stand firm and cleanse yourself. If you run away your beauty will be lost.

Without the sheikh as a mirror you will never be able to see your true self. If you run from the sheikh it will be difficult for you to be happy. Clearing yourself will be difficult, no doubt, but do you think that you will find peace if you run away? You will have difficulties wherever you go. Your life will become distasteful, and with these added difficulties you may end up going crazy. If you do not reflect on this, if you become confused and afraid and think, "What is this? I must run away," then your life will end without peace. You must hold on. If you can persevere and cleanse every part of yourself, then you will become exalted and gain peace beyond peace, tranquillity beyond tranquillity, justice beyond justice, compassion beyond compassion, unity beyond unity, patience beyond patience, and tolerance beyond tolerance.

My precious jeweled lights, while the sheikh is clearing you, he may scold you at times. But you must withstand it and hold on, so that you can see that path of peace. You must remain steadfast and in that state try to find peace.

My love you, my precious children. In your life the sheikh is a mirror for your *qalb,* your innermost heart. When you look in that mirror it will immediately show you every defect in your wisdom, your actions, words, thoughts, and qualities. This process will be as distasteful to you as bathing is to the dog. It will be like fire hissing when water is poured over it. When you use one thing to combat another it is always difficult. But during that time of difficulty you must use your wisdom. You need to understand what it is that is causing the problem and say, "I must join the sheikh and drive these things away. I must get rid of these. If I hold onto such things, it will be difficult for me and for those near me. With faith, certitude, and determination, I must drive them away." If you can behave in this way and establish such a state, then you will realize peace, happiness, and tranquillity in your life. The kingdom of God will be yours. The wealth of this world, the world of the soul, and the divine world of God will be yours.

You must realize that everything, even the sky, the sun, and the moon, lives in sorrow. One is always blocking the other. The clouds cast shadows over the sky, occluding the moon and stars. One thing is always occluding and changing the other. When this happens, they suffer. One person beats another, then that one beats another, and so on. Which one of them has peace?

A bull likes to eat grass but man likes to cut the grass. Does the bull have peace? Does the crop have peace? Does a flower have peace? No creation can ever have peace. Do you think that mind and desire can have peace? This can never happen. If you want peace, then you must be in a place where peace can be found.

Only if one stands directly under a tree will he

experience the comfort and shelter of its shade. Like this, when the heat of illusion, of attachment to the elements, desire, races, sects, and colors comes to burn you, if you are in the shade of a sheikh, you will find comfort and overcome the difficulty safely. Like the shade of a tree, the shade of the sheikh can give you peace. This peace is greater than the heat of the world. When you run from the heat, the sorrow, loss, and illusions of the world, if you can find such a tree and stand beneath it, you will have peace and comfort. This is why the sheikh exists.

Some of you might come to see the sheikh and then go away thinking, "I have seen a sheikh." You will come, finish the matter, and leave. Afterward, good or bad may come to you. You may experience peace for a while, but later desires will come to you once again. After a while a dog may come to you, or you may join a group of dogs, all of whom will try to bite you. If you join a group of demons, they will try to drink your blood. If you join a group of monkeys, they will chatter, shriek, and bite you. Is that the fault of the sheikh? No.

As long as you remain in the shade of the sheikh, it will be good. That will be a path open to truth, a path open to God. But if you join these animals, you will experience trouble and sorrow. If you run away from the sheikh and are caught by all the animals, birds, vampires, and demons, they will try to bite you. These are the difficulties you cause yourself when you deviate from the path. It is not the fault of the sheikh.

When you miss your path, mind and desire will

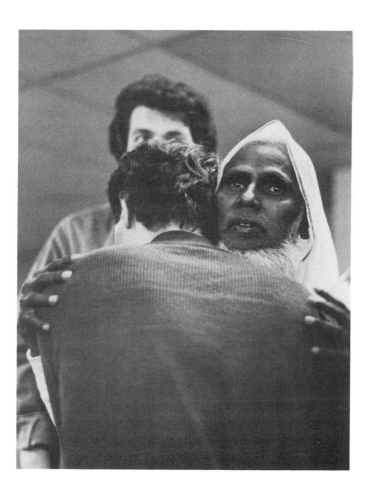

lead you away and bring you sorrow. Just as you find shade only under a tree, to find peace you must stay with the sheikh and solve these difficulties. This is what you must do, my precious children.

A monkey carries its baby close to its body wherever it goes. When things are peaceful, the baby may roam at a safe distance from the mother, but when danger is imminent, it will run and cling to the mother. Then the mother will jump from tree to tree, carrying the baby to safety. No matter how far the mother has to leap, the baby will not let go. It clings so tightly that no harm can come to it unless the mother herself is wounded. The little one is protected as long as it does not let go of the mother.

Similarly, if you hold on tightly to the *qalb* of the sheikh, then when any danger comes he will jump away from it and save you. If you cling to his heart, no danger will come to you. Only if the sheikh is in danger will you be in danger. Everything depends on how you cling to the sheikh. If you let go, you are the one who is responsible.

Now, it is also said that if a baby monkey loses its hold on the mother and falls, no other monkey will take it within its fold. It will be bitten and beaten and will die alone. Like that, if you let go of the sheikh you will never come within God's fold. God will never take you to paradise. If you separate from the truth, you will not be included in that one group, that one family to whom paradise is due. Because you have lost your hold, you will be lost in the world. As long as you are in that state, God and the kingdom of God will not accept you; that one family of the children of

God will not accept you into their fold.

If a baby monkey holds onto its mother so tightly, then how tightly should you hold onto the sheikh? If you hold onto the heart of an *insān kāmil* and remain there, you will never slip and no danger will come to you. Only if danger comes to the *kāmil sheikh* will danger come to you. Even then he will give his life for you. If someone shoots at the monkey, it is the mother who will receive the bullet and die, for she will protect the baby with her own body. Like that, if, under all circumstances, you hold onto the sheikh's heart with the grip of faith, certitude, and determination, you will not slip. That is the grip of *imān*. The baby monkey holds onto its mother with a firm grip, and we should hold onto the sheikh with the firm grip of faith. If you can hold onto the sheikh in this manner, you will never be in danger.

In this one way man and the monkey are similar. Within man, however, there are the qualities of God, the beauty of God, the actions, justice, and conscience of God, the light of God, and the radiance of God. Only if you hold onto these good qualities will you be successful. Therefore, you must stay with the sheikh and hold onto him without falling. If you can hold onto the sheikh and to that truth, it will save you. Each one of you must reflect on this. If the disciples have that grip of faith and certitude on the father's heart, they will never fall. It is difficult. To develop that conduct, those actions, and those qualities of love, compassion, patience, tolerance, peacefulness, and equality—to gain that grip and establish that state of peacefulness is indeed difficult.

It is easy for a child to put dirt on its head and roll playfully in the mud or sand, but it is difficult for the mother to bathe and cleanse the child. All the games that you play are very easy, but to bathe and cleanse you, to wash your clothes and the dirt from your head, and to make you beautiful is very difficult. The difficulties that a sheikh has in bringing up his disciples are a hundred times more difficult than those of a mother. You are always rolling in impurities, sin, fire, and hell. It is a very difficult task for the sheikh to take you and bathe you every time you dirty yourself. You do not experience the difficulties that the sheikh undergoes; it is not difficult for you, so at least try to hold onto him like the baby monkey.

If you can hold on with the grip of faith, certitude, and determination, then you can attain the correct state. That is the only way you can be protected from danger. Otherwise, when you put sand on your head and it gets in your eyes, you will cry. When you roll in the mud, slip, and hurt yourself, you will shout. It is you who has taken the sand and put it on yourself; it is not the fault of the sand or the mud. You are causing difficulty for the sheikh, not for yourself.

If your hold is correct and your heart is right, the sheikh will protect you from these dangers. If danger is imminent, the sheikh will immediately leap away and take you with him. This is how you can escape. Those who do so are the real disciples of the sheikh. He is the one who can counter your dangers and give you peace and equality. Then you will become children who will realize peace. But without this grip, no matter how long you remain with the sheikh, you will always be a victim to demons, devils, monkeys, maya, dogs, illusions, mantras, darkness, the elements, and satan. They will always be sucking your blood.

Many birds, four-legged animals, and reptiles will flee in the face of danger, leaving their babies behind. The infants will try to follow, but they will be left behind for the predator to kill. There are human beings who, like these animals, run to save themselves. There may even be sheikhs and *sayyids* who will try to save themselves first in the face of danger by running away and asking you to follow. In the face of illness or danger they will only think of saving themselves. But a true sheikh is one who will give even himself to save his children. If the sheikh is an *insān kāmil*, will he not do at least the work that a monkey does? If a monkey will do this, how much more will the sheikh do? He will protect his children far more than the monkey will.

The children must embrace the sheikh with the hands of love and faith. These physical hands might let go in certain situations, but the hands of faith and love will never let go. Children who have that love will correct themselves and go on the right path.

When one of his loving children makes a mistake, at first the sheikh will just watch for a while, but if the child continues to repeat that fault, the sheikh will hit the child with the cane of wisdom. His love will embrace you while wisdom beats you and tries to correct you. When wisdom strikes, love will not be hurt, but ignorance and lack of wisdom will feel the blow.

Some children run away when their ignorance is

hurt. If their hands of love and faith are not strong, at one time or another they will let go. But if that love and faith is strong in their hearts, they will never let go no matter what happens. When their mistakes are hit with wisdom, they will not feel hurt. They will listen, nod their heads in acceptance, and say, "I will try not to do that again." They will think about it and then hold on even tighter with the hand of love.

Consider the example of a mother hen. A hen will allow her chicks to run about and play. But when an enemy approaches, she warns them, "Come! Come quickly!" and they must immediately run and hide beneath her wings. Only then can she protect her chicks. The hen warns, "A hawk is above, watching and waiting to kill you!" The mother calls to her chicks and pecks them. If the chicks run away from her when she pecks them, they are in serious danger; they could easily be caught and killed by the hawk.

A real father who has true love protects his children just as the mother hen protects her chicks. He protects his children from the evils of the world, from the poisons of life, from illusion, from desire, and from evil. A loving father of wisdom warns you and calls out to protect you from the dangers that may harm you. If a child does not respond to his call, then he hits that child with wisdom. If you become angry because of this and run away that is your fault, and you will suffer from your actions. This is how the loving father of wisdom tries to protect you from the accidents of the world, from the five senses, and from your mind.

If your hold on faith and love is not strong, the

father will hit you, either lightly or hard; he will hit you to strengthen you. If your hold is loose, you let go and run away in times of danger or personal difficulty. Then you will definitely suffer, and it will be your own fault. A child who holds on correctly with love will run closer to his father in these moments just as a chick runs to its mother. The more its mother pecks, the quicker it hurries to seek shelter under her wings. Similarly, when you realize this and seek shelter in your father, you will be saved from the evils of life.

This is how faith and love work. They touch the heart and hold onto it. This is the truth. This is how a true father will be. Such love and faith do not exist in everyone; it is very rare. Selfish love and selfish affection will release their hold. A selfish mother, father, guru, or sheikh might let go when there is difficulty or when the relationship is no longer suitable to them. Only a father who has selfless love will hold on and try to help you no matter what happens.

Consider another example. A fish knows the depth of the well it lives in. The insects, however, live only on the surface. These insects have four legs, and their feet are shaped like shoes. They walk on the water and touch the surface, but they know nothing about the depth of the well. At any moment a fish can come up from beneath and devour them. The insects know nothing about the fish below.

Like that, you are walking on the surface of the pond of illusion. You should not think that you know its secrets. You do not know the secrets of maya. You do not know what lies below, in its depths. The wisdom you have learned is like that of the insect that skids along on the surface of a life of illusion. A fish can come up from beneath and catch you at any time. It will hide in the mud and then suddenly grab you.

A true man with real wisdom will know what is above and below. A father of wisdom, a sheikh, will know both the surface and depth of maya, like the fish knows the depth of the water. A father of wisdom will know what is deep and what is shallow in life. You cannot know the secrets which lie in the depths or the accidents that might occur in your life. But a true father will know and he will warn you.

When you see a danger in front of you, you retreat. When you see something behind you, you run forward. That is all you can do. Eventually, you will be caught between the two. You will run and run until you are cornered. You do not know how to find out what is ahead of you or what lies behind you. But a true father will know and he will warn you. Even before you begin your journey, a wise man of experience will know what lies ahead. He will tell you, "These are the dangers on this path. These are the dangers on that path. If you go this way you can escape." He might say, "Follow me, I will take you." Then you can escape.

If you think you know the way, when danger appears behind you, you will immediately run forward into the darkness. But then if danger appears in front of you, you will be trapped. Even if you have a gun you will be unable to use it. You will drop it out of fear. Then the one who comes to attack you will use that very gun to kill you.

You need the protection of a wise father to help you escape from these accidents. You need a good man to help you, a wise man with good qualities who knows. Think about this, all of you.

With faith, certitude, and determination, keep that unfailing grip on the heart of the sheikh. Then you will receive the milk of wisdom and grace. He will feed you with that milk of grace which can heal your hunger, illness, old age, and death. He will feed you with that true milk of grace and wisdom. He will give that honey, and you will know that taste. If you hold onto the sheikh and drink that milk and honey, you will realize the exaltedness of your life. You will know peace and happiness; you will derive God's qualities and the light of heaven. In this way, you must stay with the sheikh and accept his qualities, his wisdom, and his actions. If you grow in this way you can progess. But if you do not have this grip, your life will be filled with difficulties. Each one of the children must think about this. This is what the connection between the sheikh and the disciple should be like.

My love you, my children, my sons, my daughters, my brothers, my sisters—each one of you should think about this. If you can behave in this manner you will be the children of God, and you will realize peace. *Āmīn*.

Be Observant

On the path of God, whether we are performing our worldly duties or following the sheikh, we must constantly be like first-rate, observant detectives.

Once there was a police station which had a vacancy for a detective. Many people applied for the job, and they were all led upstairs by a senior officer. When each one was asked what he had observed along the way, only one applicant could describe the route, the number of turns, and other identifying signs. He alone had counted the one hundred and twenty-eight steps. The others had blindly followed the senior officer without noticing anything.

In the same way, there are many steps for us to climb while following the sheikh. It is our job to carefully observe each point along the way. In the world there are six steps or levels of consciousness: feeling, awareness, intellect, judgment, wisdom, and divine analytic wisdom. The sheikh is constantly checking these steps of our wisdom. If you are trying to climb this mountain to attain that state, the sheikh will say, "All right, if this is what you want, then come along."

You must also climb the five steps of earth, fire, water, air, and ether. On the journey of your life you must surmount and conquer each one. If you wish to do this, the sheikh will begin the climb and ask you to follow closely behind. It is your job to observe carefully each point along your path. First is the earth, your body. What are its signs? What is its state? What does it do? What explanation does it give? You must study all these points.

Secondly, when you turn left you will come upon the fire of your hunger. You must observe what there is to be seen in this; you must understand what needs to be understood. Then when you turn to the right you come to the third step, air. What do the gases and vapors do to the body? What does air do? Does it fatigue you? Does it make you breathless or tired? How does this air work within you? What about the breath, the gases, the spiritual worships, magics, and tricks? How do they function? Observe these signs attentively and understand point by point.

At the fourth turn you come to water: the clouds, the things in your life which are capable of torporizing your wisdom and judgment. Creation and torpor are water. What do these torpors do? In what way are they torpid? How do they come? How does desire hypnotize? How does the mind hypnotize? In what way does this state come to you? You must understand the point.

The fifth turn, to the right, is maya, or illusion.

That is the ether. What is the state of your destiny, your *nasīb,* your life's limit? What effect does maya have upon you? How many forms does illusion take? What beauty does it show you? What section does it reveal? You must understand every point in this step.

The sixth step goes straight through to the right. This is the path that leads to the west. At the sixth level, you must analyze and discriminate between right and wrong, good and bad. There you will learn to say, "This is bad and must be discarded. This is good. We must keep it." You must understand everything on this path.

Once you have separated right from wrong and have completed the sixth level, you will find yourself on a plateau. Then the sheikh will ask, "All right, you have climbed this far. Now what is your aim? What do you need? Do you want status or position? Was it for the sake of position that you came here? What wondrous things did you see along the way? What did you observe as you climbed the steps?"

You must answer him carefully. If you sputter meaningless words you will not receive that state because you failed to understand the point. If you say, "Oh, I didn't see anything," he will ask, "In that case, how did you manage to climb to this point? How many steps were there? How many corners? Which way did you turn after each point?" If again you answer, "Oh I didn't pay attention, I was merely following you blindly. I didn't observe anything," he will say, "Is that so? Then you have lost your point."

The subtle one of the group will answer, "Yes, I

noticed everything. I took this many steps, then turned to the left, saw certain signs, took so many more steps, and turned to the right where I saw these identifying signs. When I turned to the left again, it was like this, and then when I turned to the right it was like this. In all, there were one hundred and twenty-eight steps and six corners or turns. The initial and final paths were both straight; in between were these five corners."

The sheikh will reply, "That is correct. You are the one who is worthy of attaining the seventh step called *perr-arivu*. You are worthy enough to see this divine luminous wisdom." Then the sheikh will reveal to you the light of the *nūr,* the resplendence of Allah. "You alone are fit to see this. Go there now and continue your studies."

Thus, as you walk behind the sheikh, you must observe each and every point—what you see as you progress, what you observe in his words and his actions, what he does and what he looks at. Through this observation you must recognize what you yourself must see and do. As you watch, you must pay attention to all these things. This is the map, this is *gnānam.* You must understand everything and carry this map as you follow him. Whenever he asks you a question, you must be able to answer.

If you walk behind him carelessly, smoking a cigarette and talking, you will lose the point of your journey. It is a very subtle point. On this path, as you journey from birth to death, until Judgment Day, there are so many points and signs that need to be seen and understood. It is only if you grasp these points that you will be an adept person who can be given that station of Man-God. Then in God's kingdom, as a true human being, as God's child, you can do His duty and function in that state of service. But if you are not attentive and follow behind the sheikh without being watchful, then your wisdom will have no clarity.

On your path there are also the four steps of *tānum, nītanum, avatānum,* and *gnānam.* The first, *tānum,* is the complete surrender of yourself. *Nītanum* is concentration and focus, walking very carefully on this dangerous path. *Avatānum* is perfect balance, watching very closely that you do not topple to one side or the other when the wind, mind, desire, maya, money, and bloodties push against you. *Avatānum* is the perfect balance on the path which is sharper than the edge of a sword. To walk along it is certainly very difficult. If your attention lapses you may stray or fall. But if you succeed in walking that sharp edge, then you will reach the station of *gnānam.*

If you can succeed in crossing, you will attain that state of wisdom. Only then will you be capable of completing the duties you were assigned. If you want to perform these duties so that you can satisfy people's needs, comfort their minds, dispel their worries, and give them peace, then as you walk behind your sheikh you must pay close attention day and night to his every breath. Take account and grasp each point. Go within and analyze his every word. Go within and analyze his every look. See what that look means. Observe how the sheikh is walking, and from this discern if there are snakes or scorpions about. Only if you can evaluate all this while walking behind the sheikh will you be given that state. Then he will say, "Oh yes, you are certainly fit for this path," and he will point you to that station.

This world is a map, and you are the detective who must follow the clues and catch the thieves. This world is filled with thieves like mind and desire, the five elements, attachments, cravings, religions, caste differences, racial and color differences, property, wealth and riches, status and exalted positions. All these dwell within the body, within the mind, and within the world. They are all rogues. How are you going to catch them and lock them up? Earth, fire, water, air, ether, arrogance, karma, and maya; *tārahan, singhan,* and *sūran;* anger, miserliness, attachments, fanaticism and envy; intoxicants, lust, theft, murder, and falsehood; the division between 'you' and 'I', the religious and racial differences are all thieves trying to steal that wealth which belongs to God. They have strayed from God's justice but are trying to steal His wealth. They have strayed from compassion, from God's love, and from unity. They steal for the sake of self-gain.

So how do you think you can capture these rogues? You have to be very, very attentive and observant of each step as you walk along. If you are not alert and watchful, you will never succeed in arresting these thieves who live in your kingdom. In fact, they might catch you! They might even kill you. Therefore, make it your responsibility to catch these rogues and imprison them. If you can subdue and arrest them, you can bring the justice, peace, and tranquillity of God's kingdom to all lives.

If you want to be appointed to that station, if you want to bring His state to all lives, then you need the subtle attentiveness, subtle actions, and the qualities required to catch all these thieves. Only then will you be qualified to present yourself for the examination. Then, having studied everything with the sheikh and having taken the right points, you can instruct others in God's kingdom and comfort them. However, if you claim you are following the sheikh, while in fact you have not observed or heard anything, then your life will have been in vain. If you are not alert, the rogues might grab you and carry you away; demons and maya might carry you off.

Those of you who are following the sheikh and who aspire to an exalted station have to reflect upon this. Do you understand? To attain that station, how very careful we must be, how attentive and observant. My love you my sons, daughters, and grandchildren. Think about what we must accomplish on this path and how we can make ourselves worthy of that appointment. May God help you. May He give you the strength, the wisdom, and the *imān* to attain that high station. *Āmīn.*

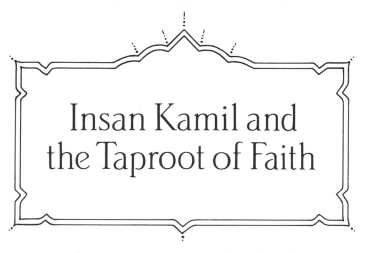

Insan Kamil and the Taproot of Faith

From time to time in each child's life he feels confused, his mind wavers, and he becomes tired. If this weariness comes when you are in a place of truth and justice, or even if you have gone to God Himself, it is because your faith is not strong enough. This tiredness comes because your certitude in that Power is not strong. Truth must have faith in truth. Justice must speak justice and have faith in justice. God's qualities must have trust and faith in God.

Let us look at a tree as an example. A tree has one main root that goes deep into the earth and many supporting roots that spread along the surface. When there is a storm or heavy rain, the supporting roots might be uprooted. It is the main root, the taproot, that protects the tree from falling. Though storms may toss the tree from side to side, this supreme root will maintain the balance, supporting the tree and holding it firm.

In the same way, man's surface roots are the mind and the five elements. But faith in God, firm

101

certitude, wisdom, determination, and God's qualities compose the taproot that must penetrate deeply into truth. If you have that supreme root and it has fixed itself firmly in this truth, then fatigue and wavering of the mind will not come to you. If that root has penetrated deep into the truth, then when the storms of mind and desire, bloodties, religions, colors, race, property, love, illusion, darkness, hunger, old age, disease, and death come to attack you, your firm faith in God will support you, just as the taproot supports the tree. The storms that mind, desire, and maya bring will beat against you, but they will pass by if that faith in God is firm.

However, if this strong root is not there, if this firm faith in God is not present and the tree is depending on the surface roots only, it will be easily uprooted by the storms and gales. If man expects support from earth, fire, water, air, and ether, he will not get it. People consider the elements as gods, but they do not have the power of God. These five elements are not dependable and may change when suffering and sorrow come. All the gods created by the five elements, the energies, and maya will run when sorrow comes to attack you. These gods will not support you; they will not be there permanently to help you. The five elements, your intellect, awareness, and feeling will all change. If sadness comes you will lose your awareness. When you suffer you will lose your consciousness, and when still more suffering comes, you will lose your intellect. All these things which are supporting you now cannot last when suffering comes. Their power is limited. You cannot depend on their help.

We need the abiding, permanent help of God. We must have certitude, determination, and faith deeply rooted in that One God. If we have that deep taproot of faith, it will always support us. These other *saktis* and elements will change, but the power of God never changes.

If you do not have strong faith in God, you will never be able to find peace when the storms of tiredness, doubt, and confusion repeatedly attack and affect you. It is because this taproot is weak and has not taken firm root that you experience all this suffering and fatigue. You have not found peace in your life or peace on God's path, because you have not established this state of firm faith.

A tree which has its taproot firmly fixed is also able to draw the necessary water and nutrients from the soil. It then flowers, bears fruits, and is of benefit to others. Because the taproot has fixed itself firmly, deep in the soil, the tree is able not only to withstand the storms but also to nourish itself from the source. Through finding its own food and benefiting others with its fruits, it has peace in life.

In the same way, man can receive food for the freedom of his soul and through that be of benefit to others. If man has that taproot of faith firmly implanted in God, he can find peace. He finds peace because he is able to do both duties: duty to his own soul and duty to others. Wherever he is, he can derive his power from God and receive his nourishment from this power.

But, children, all those who have a body made of

the five elements must undergo suffering. Even though you might be one who has cut away the attachments to the world and the connection to the five elements, nevertheless all those who have a body of these elements will experience difficulty. Only God who has no form does not experience this suffering. I too feel tired just as you do. Why? Because even when you are in a place of truth, there are difficulties. Even for one on the path of God, difficulties can arise through the connection to one's children. When troubles come to the children, then one of truth asks, "O God, why are You giving these difficulties to the children? Protect them." The poverty, illnesses, sorrows, and hunger of a child affect the wise man also. These sorrows do affect a man of truth. Because of his physical body, he is shaken a little. Because he has firm faith in God, however, it affects him for only a second or two and then passes. But it does affect him for that moment.

Even though he has given up attachment to the world, the attachment to his children on this path affects him. Once he gives up that attachment, then he is God. But as long as he has this attachment to take God's children back to God, he is man. Although he is an *insān kāmil,* a representative of God, he still has this attachment to take the children of God back to God and the truth. Because of this, he also has a connection to all the accidents and difficulties that befall his children on this path.

When disease, disturbances from the world, sorrow, the five elements, mind, and desire come to attack one of his children, and the wise man realizes

104

that the child has fallen, he has to lift that child up, care for him, and carry that child with him. That work is a little difficult, and at such times he undergoes suffering. Until he opens that path and hands you over to God's responsibility, difficulties will come. Until that time, he has to take you carefully, with strong faith. He does not have the world within him, but he is attached to taking you to God and giving you the freedom of your soul. Because of this attachment he has to share your suffering.

All those born in this world with the form of the five elements undergo disturbances and sorrow. God alone is the exception. Like all of you, I too have a physical body. God does not have such a body, so for Him it is easy. You must understand this. With every thought you have, sorrows can come to you. They come and they go, but we must have firm faith and certitude in God. When you are affected by the pull of your connections to caste, lust, anger, bloodties, colors, and religion, you feel tired. This weariness does not come from God. It comes because your taproot is not strong enough. If we do not have this strength, we cannot find peace either for ourselves or for others.

If the root of a tree has grown deeply into the earth and the branches have grown strong, we can take hold of those branches, climb the tree, and pluck the fruits. But if we hold onto a branch of maya, we will not be able to climb. Such branches might appear strong; they might appear to have glittering fruits, but it is only a show. If we grab hold of those illusory branches, we will fall. If we use wisdom and certitude, however, we will not grab onto those branches of maya which will cause us danger. Faith in God is the real strength, and the fruit on the branch of God's truth is the true fruit. If we do not take our fruit from the branch of God's truth, if instead we pluck a fruit from the glittering branches of maya, magic, and mesmerism, if we hold onto LSD, opium, and marijuana, we will fall down. If we hold onto differences of religion and race, we will experience many difficulties and sorrows which will cause us to waver. But if we hold onto the strong branch of truth, we can eat the true, beautiful fruits of grace.

My children, my love you. We have to think about this. You must firmly establish your certitude and faith in God. If you have the strength of that faith within you, storms and gales will come to push and sway you, but then they will pass on. If your faith and certitude is weak, however, they will toss you around and shake you up.

The tree finds peace through securing its own nourishment and through doing its duty to God by helping others. If you do not have this strength of faith in God, you will find neither peace in your soul nor peace in the world. In this present-day world, if you are looking for peace and truth in your life and freedom for your soul, it is here with the sheikh that you can attain this state. If you have the certitude, faith, determination, and good qualities, there may be room for you here to attain this peace. There is a place for you here to learn peace, both for this world and for the freedom of your soul. You must think about this.

However, if instead you are looking for miracles, you can find them within every creation. Crocodiles, tigers, lions, poisonous snakes, and even some poisonous ants can make man suffer with their miracles. Fire, earth, water, air, ether, illusion, darkness—all have the power to make man suffer. Fire can burn down a house, water can destroy the world, air can tear things apart, one earthquake can destroy a whole city, one blast of thunder and lightning can strike and shake everything up. The elements have the power to do all this. These are indeed miracles. If a snake bites a man, the man suffers and dies. A tiger can drink a man's blood and eat his liver. These are their miracles. To attack another man is a miracle. To make him suffer and to take pride in that is a miracle. To destroy another man to establish your pride and superiority is a miracle. But that is not the true miracle.

My love you, my children. To find peace within yourself is the real miracle. To find peace in your life of wisdom and your life in the world is truly a miracle. This is something no man can accomplish alone. It is very difficult. If you can live without hurting other lives, without killing any life, without causing suffering to any life, without destroying anything; if you can give peace to all lives—that is how you can find peace for your own soul and your own life. You must find peace for yourself and then give that benefit to all other beings. That is the real miracle. That is the miracle you must see within yourself. But no man can do this on his own. Man can do everything else, but he cannot do this.

To control the mind and to keep still is indeed most difficult. To find peace both in the world and in your soul, you need to learn God's qualities and the grace of His wisdom. It is not necessary to search for miracles. All the miracles are within you. To praise yourself, saying, "I am great, you are great, I am God," is not real. To find peace within yourself is real. That is the greatest miracle.

You yourself know what is good or bad, what is right or wrong. Whenever you have done something wrong, a warning within you will say, "Why did you scold him? Why did you hit him? What you did was wrong." The judgment of right and wrong is within you. The judgment and justice of whatever you have done is made known to you by wisdom. You must learn to recognize this warning within.

You need not go to a courtroom; the court of justice is within you. You need not search for judgment from anywhere else; the judgment is within you. You need not look for hell or heaven somewhere else; both exist within you. Everything is within you. Truth is not somewhere else, it is within. You can understand everything you need to know, for it is all within you.

You must learn to recognize this warning that is within you. To make this function properly, you need a wise man. You need God's qualities and the grace of God's wisdom. It is wisdom that you must search for. To find peace in both worlds you need this clarity. You must find a wise man with God's qualities and learn from him.

Consider another point. Motors work at different

speeds. Some engines might rotate ten thousand times per minute, others twenty thousand times, and still others fifty thousand. The power of the motor is determined by the speed of rotation. It is like that on the path of God. The speed and subtlety of your wisdom and the determination of your faith cause light to come from that Power. The light shines when your wisdom works swiftly. It is this speed which allows the current to emerge. It is also important that the wisdom be strong, otherwise if the speed is excessive the motor will break. On the other hand, if the speed is deficient, the current cannot pass through and again the motor will break. Each machine has a specific speed and limit within which the motor must rotate. If we go beyond that limit the motor will break. We must learn the limit and know how the engine works.

Like the motor, God is a power which provides light to the whole world and dispels all darkness. His power stations are the *insān kāmils,* the true human beings, the wise men. God is the source of light which dispels the darkness of the mind and the darkness of life. Grace, wisdom, and His qualities come from that main source, and He sends that power down to these transmitting stations, the *insān kāmils,* His representatives. The wise man must receive and distribute this power. To dispel your darkness and give you peace in life, an *insān kāmil* must derive his supply from the main source and then distribute it to you. He receives the wisdom, truth, and qualities from that main source and supplies them to others. He takes the point and the truth and dispels the darkness of life and the darkness of maya. He supplies the wisdom to help others rid themselves of the sorrows and difficulties that come into their lives.

God knows everything. There is nothing that God does not know. But for Him, nothing would move. There is no place where He does not exist. All souls have a connection to Him; all truth, all good deeds, everything has a connection to God and He has a connection to everything. There is nothing He does not know, nothing He does not understand. He gives food to the weeds, to the grass, to the toad under a stone, and to the fetus in the womb. So what is there for us to ask of God? If you were to ask God for something, what could you ask for? There is no need to ask for anything. He knows everything.

We must look into our own hearts and ask why we have this suffering. We must find the cause of our sorrow and correct ourselves. We must find the cure for our suffering. It is ourselves we must question. This is not God's fault. This suffering and weariness is caused by some connection within us, so we must ask ourselves why this has happened. If something has gone wrong, it is because of what we have within us. We must discover the reason and correct ourselves. There is nothing to ask of God.

God does not hurt anyone. His work is to create, protect, and sustain. But if you find that you are unable to bear something, if there is nothing you can do or avoid doing to end this suffering, if it is beyond your wisdom and you cannot deal with it anymore—then surrender. If you cannot handle it with your wisdom or your qualities, then put up your hands in surrender, saying, "There is nothing I can do, O God. I am unable to do anything with my wisdom or my qualities. I am unable to help myself. You must help me."

All the sorrows, all the disturbances that come to us are caused by ourselves, and so we must correct our own faults. It is our work to clean what we have dirtied. When you go to the bathroom, you must clean yourself. You have to clean your bed. You have to clean the earth before you sleep on it. It is your own fault if you just lie down on the ground and the ants and the insects bite you.

God has given you two eyes, two ears, two nostrils, a mouth, and two openings below. He has given you these so that you can understand. It is your fault if you fail. All these are given to you, and you must understand your duty and your state. But without doing your work, you fail and then you ask, "Is God testing me? Is God punishing me, is He angry with me?" No, it is all your own fault. When you have corrected your faults, you will become clear. There is nothing more we need ask from God. You do not have to ask, "Oh God, please forgive me." If we can correct the mistakes we have made, then we are forgiven. No matter what difficulty, illness, or suffering comes to us, it comes because of our actions. To know this we need the clarity of faith, wisdom, and God's qualities.

What use is there in saying, "Oh God protect us, help us." God's duty is to create, protect, and sustain, and He is doing it. And you must do your duty;

then you will find peace. If you know what your duty is and do it, your life will be heaven. Your life will be the kingdom of heaven; there will be no kingdom of hell for you. The freedom of your soul and the freedom of your lives will be your heaven. Then you will be God's children.

We have to understand freedom, peacefulness, and unity. To know this is wisdom, God's qualities, and truth. This is why you need a true man, an *insān kāmil*, to transmit the energy to power your motor. You need a man of truth; you need his wisdom, his qualities, and his actions. In this century, this is a good place for you to receive this kind of help. Here, you might be able to receive clarity and wisdom. But you need faith. You need faith to attain what you are searching for. You must have that faith, certitude, and determination, and you must learn that from one who has wisdom and these qualities.

For peacefulness to come to you, you must receive it from someone who has peacefulness. You must receive patience from one who has patience. You must receive justice from one who has justice. Then you will find peace for your life and for your soul. You will have peace in this world and in the next. The peace that you find within yourself is the only true miracle. This is what you must search for. My love you. Understand this. *Āmīn.* May God help us.

Glossary

(A) indicates an Arabic word. (T) indicates Tamil

agnānam (T) Ignorance; worldly or materialistic wisdom; speech from the level of the intellect. See also: *gnānam.*

aiyō! (T) An exclamatory expression, "Oh no!"

ākhir (A) The hereafter; the next world; the kingdom of God.

al-hamdu lillāh (A) "All praise is to You." Allah is the glory and greatness that deserves all praise. "You are the One responsible for the appearance of all creations. Whatever appears, whatever disappears, whatever receives benefit or loss—all is Yours. I have surrendered everything into Your hands. I remain with hands outstretched, empty, and helpless. Whatever is happening and whatever is going to happen is all Your responsibility." Lit.: All praise belongs to Allah!

Āmīn (A) So be it. May He make this complete.

arwāh (A) The world of the pure soul, where all souls are performing *tasbīh* [prayers of praise] to God; the period when the souls were manifested and then scattered all over.

As-salāmu 'alaikum wa Rahmatullāhi wa barakātuhu kulluhu (A) May the peace of God and His beneficence be upon all of you!

avatānum (T)   Focus; perfect balance.

awwal (A)   The creation of all forms; the stage at which the soul became surrounded by form and each creation took form; the stage at which the souls of the six kinds of lives [earth-life, fire-life, water-life, air-life, ether-life, and light-life] were placed in their respective forms. Allah creates forms and then places that 'trust property' that is life within those forms.

Bismillāhir-Rahmānir-Rahīm (A)   In the name of God, Most Merciful, Most Compassionate. *Bismillāh:* Allah is the first and the last. The One with the beginning and the One without beginning. He is the One who is the cause for creation and for the absence of creation, the cause for the beginning and the beginningless.

   Ar-Rahmān: He is the King. He is the Nourisher, the One who gives food. He is the Compassionate One. He is the One who protects the creations. He is the Beneficent One.

   Ar-Rahīm: He is the One who redeems; the One who protects from evil, who preserves and who confers eternal bliss; the Savior. On the day of judgment and on the day of inquiry and on all days from the day of the beginning, He protects and brings His creations back to Himself.

dunyā (A)   The earth world in which we live; the world of physical existence; the darkness which separated from Allah at the time when the light of the *Nūr* Muhammad manifested from within Allah.

firdaus (A)   The eighth heaven, Allah's house of infinite magnitude and perfect purity.

gnānam (T)   Divine analytic wisdom. Allah has placed within the body of man the wealth of all the eighteen thousand universes. Man holds within his hands: hell and heaven, good and evil [*khair* and *sharr*], the secret and the manifestations [*sirr* and *sifāt*], the essence and the manifestations [*dhāt* and *sifāt*], and that which is forbidden and that which is permissible [*harām* and *halāl*]. Allah has placed within him the wealth of the world, of heaven and hell; the wealth of the *nafs* [base desires]; the wealth of satan; the wealth which desire desires; the treasure which earth desires, which water desires, which fire desires, or which the air and the spirits desire; and the treasures which illusion [maya] desires.

If man can throw away all these treasures and take within him only the treasure called Allah and His qualities and actions, His conduct and behavior, if he makes Allah the only treasure and completeness for him, that is the state of *gnānam*.

What treasure is there other than Allah? All the rest is *agnānam* [ignorance] and *poignānam* [false wisdom]. *Agnānam* is the *gnānam* of the world. False wisdom is the *gnānam* of darkness, the speech which one speaks in the torpor and intoxication of darkness. *Agnānam* is the speech from the intellect; *vingnānam* [scientific wisdom] is the explanation given by the subtle intellect. *Meignānam* is to know and understand. *Meignānam* is from Allah's words; it is to know and understand through that word and to eliminate all that is evil. Other than Him there is no treasure. To know that everything other than Him is perishable and destructible and to throw them all away—that is *meignānam*.

gnāna sheikh (T)   A sheikh who has attained the state of *gnānam;* one who can point the way to God; a truly realized human being. See: *gnānam*.

hadīth (A)   In Islam, a traditional story spoken by the prophets. These are the words or commands of Allah which were received by Prophet Muhammad (*Sal.*) and the other prophets and were conveyed and demonstrated to the people. Also *hadīth qudsī:* the words of Allah that were given directly to the prophets without the Angel Gabriel (*A.S.*) as an intermediary. Sometimes a story about the prophets.

hayāt (A)　The plenitude of man's eternal life; the splendor of the completeness of life; the *rūh* or the soul of the splendor of man's life.

'ilm (A)　Divine knowledge; the ocean of knowledge; the ocean of grace.

imān (A)　Absolute, complete and unshakable faith, certitude and determination that God alone exists; the complete acceptance of the heart that God is One. See also: *sabūr,* for the five prefaces to *imān.*

indira jālam (T)　The magic tricks of maya which extend into space; the tricks of magic performed in space.

insān kāmil (A)　A perfected, God-realized being. One who has made Allah his only wealth, cutting away all the wealth of the world and the wealth sought by the mind. One who has acquired God's qualities, performs his actions accordingly, and contains himself within those qualities.

Ka'bah (A)　The cube-like building in the center of the mosque in Mecca. One of the five obligations [*furūd*] of Islam is a pilgrimage [*hajj*] to the *Ka'bah.*

Another meaning: the innermost heart or *qalb* which is the original source of prayer, the place where a true man or *insān* meets Allah face to face. Whoever brings his heart to that state of perfection and prays to God from that heart will be praying from the *Ka'bah.*

kāmil sheikh (A)　A perfected teacher. See also: *insān kāmil, gnāna sheikh.*

maya (T)　Illusion; the unreality of the visible world; the glitters seen in the darkness of illusion; the 105 million glitters seen in the darkness of the mind which result in 105 million rebirths. Maya is an energy or *sakti* which takes on various shapes, causes man to forfeit his wisdom, and hypnotizes him into a state of torpor. It can take many, many millions of hypnotic forms. And if man tries to grasp these forms with his intellect, he will see the form but he cannot catch it, for it will take on yet another form.

meignānam (T) See *gnānam*.

mubārakāt (A) The supreme, imperishable treasure of all three worlds (the beginning [*awwal*], this world [*dunyā*], and the hereafter [*ākhir*]). The wealth and the one who gives that wealth is Allah and nothing else. Lit.: The three blessings of Allah, a combination of the Tamil *mu* meaning three, and Arabic *barakāt* meaning blessings.

mu'min (A) A true believer; one of true *īmān* [absolute faith, certitude, and determination].

nafs or *nafs ammārah* (A) The seven kinds of selfish desires. That is, desires meant to satisfy one's own pleasure and comforts. All thoughts are contained within the *ammārah*. *Ammārah* is like the mother while the *nafs* are like the children. Lit.: Person, spirit, inclination, or desire.

nasīb (A) Destiny; your life's limit.

nitānum (T) Complete concentration and focus.

nūr (A) The resplendence of Allah; the plenitude of the light of Allah; the completeness of Allah's qualities. When the plenitude of all these become one and resplend as one, that is the *nūr*—that is Allah's qualities and Allah's beauty.

perr-arivu (T) Sixth level of wisdom; divine luminous wisdom.

purānas (T) Stories, usually referring to the Hindu scriptures. His Holiness speaks of the 17 *purānas* within man as the qualities of arrogance, karma, and maya; the three sons of maya, *tārahan, singhan* and *sūran;* lust, anger, miserliness, attachment, fanaticism, envy, intoxicants, obsession, theft, murder, and falsehood.

qalb (A) The heart within the heart of man; the inner-

117

most heart. His Holiness explains that there are two states for the *qalb*. One state is made of four chambers which represent Hinduism, Fire Worship, Christianity, and Islam. Inside these four chambers there is a flower, the flower of the *qalb,* which is the divine qualities of God. That is the second state, the flower of grace [*rahmat*]. God's fragrance exists only in this *qalb*.

qiblah (A)   Externally, the direction one faces in prayer. For Jews the *qiblah* is Jerusalem; for Muslims it is Mecca. But to face Allah while in prayer is the true *qiblah*. Internally, it is the throne of Allah within the heart [*qalb*].

qudrat (A)   The power of God's grace and the qualities that control all other forces.

Rabbal-'ālamīn (A)   Lord of all the universes, Allah.

rahmat (A)   God's grace; His forgiveness and compassion; His benevolence; His wealth. To all creations, He is the wealth of life [*hayāt*] and the wealth of *īmān* [absolute faith, certitude, and determination]. All the good things that man receives from God are called His *rahmat*. That is the wealth of God's plenitude.

rahmatul-'ālamīn (A)   The Mercy and Compassion of all the universes. The One who gives everything to all His creations. He makes them arise by saying, *"Kun!* [Be!]"* and then He gives whatever they need, comforts them, and rules over them.

rasūl (A)   Apostle or messenger; one who has wisdom, faith in God, and good qualities; one who behaves with respect and dignity toward his fellow men; one who has completely accepted only God and has rejected everything else; one who has accepted God's divine words, His qualities and actions, and puts them into practice. Those who from time immemorial have been giving the divine laws of God to the people and who have such a connection with God have been called a prophet [*nabī*] or a *rasūl*. *Yā Rasūl* is a name given to Prophet Muhammad (*Sal.*).

sabūr (A)   Inner patience; to go within patience, to accept it, to think and reflect within it. *Sabūr* is that patience deep within patience which comforts, soothes, and alleviates mental suffering.

    Yā Sabūr: one of the 99 names of Allah. God, who is in a state of limitless patience, forgiving the faults of His created beings and continuing to protect them.

sakti (T)   A force or energy. In the Tamil *purānas,* it also refers to the consort of Shiva.

sayyid(*s*) (A)   Descendants of Prophet Muhammad (*Sal.*). In modern times, however, the meaning has degenerated almost to an equivalent of 'Mister'.

shukūr (A)   Contentment; the state within inner patience [*sabūr*]; that which is kept within the treasure chest of patience. This is the plural form in Arabic of the word *shukr* which means gratitude and thankfulness leading to contentment. In these texts only the plural is used to avoid confusion. *Yā Shakūr*—one of the 99 beautiful names of Allah. To have *shukūr* with the help of the one who is *Yā Shakūr* is true *shukūr*. See also: *sabūr.*

siddhi (T)   Magic; miracle; supernatural abilities, commonly called miracles, obtained by devotion to and control of the elements.

singhan (T)   See: *tārahan.*

tānum (T)   Complete surrender of oneself to God.

tārahan, singhan, sūran (T)   The three sons of maya, or illusion. *Tārahan* is the trench or pathway for the sexual act, the birth canal or vagina. *Singhan* is the arrogance present at the moment when the semen is ejaculated [*karma*]. It is the quality of the lion. *Sūran* is the illusory images of the mind enjoyed at the moment of ejaculation. It is all the qualities and energies of the mind.

tawakkal-Allāh or *tawakkul* (A)   Absolute trust and surrender; handing over to God the entire responsibility for everything. Same as *Allāhu Wakīl*—You are my Trustee, my Lawyer, my Guardian. *Yā Wakīl* is one of the 99 beautiful names of Allah.

wilāyats (A)   God's power; that which has been revealed and manifested through God's actions; the miraculous names and actions of God; the powers of His attributes through which all creations came into existence.

Yā Rabbal-'ālamīn (A)   O Ruler of the universes! The Creator who nourishes and protects all of His creations forever.

OTHER BOOKS BY
M. R. BAWA MUHAIYADDEEN

Truth & Light: brief explanations

Songs of God's Grace

*The Divine Luminous Wisdom
That Dispels the Darkness*

*The Guidebook to the True Secret of the Heart
(Volumes One and Two)*

God, His Prophets and His Children

Four Steps to Pure Iman

The Wisdom of Man

A Book of God's Love

*My Love You My Children:
101 Stories for Children of All Ages*

*Come to the Secret Garden:
Sufi Tales of Wisdom*

The Golden Words of a Sufi Sheikh

*The Tasty, Economical Cookbook
(Volume Two)*

Maya Veeram or The Forces of Illusion

*Asma'ul-Husna:
The 99 Beautiful Names of Allah*

*Islam and World Peace:
Explanations of a Sufi*

A Mystical Journey

*Questions of Life / Answers of Wisdom
(Volume One)*

For free catalog or book information call:
(215) 879-8604

The central branch of the Bawa Muhaiyaddeen Fellowship is located in Philadelphia, PA. The Fellowship serves as a meeting house and as a reservoir of people and materials for all who are interested in the teachings of Bawa Muhaiyaddeen.

For information, write or call:

The Bawa Muhaiyaddeen Fellowship
5820 Overbrook Avenue
Philadelphia, Pennsylvania 19131

Telephone: (215) 879-6300

For free catalog or book information call: (215) 879-8604